ADVANCE PRAISE

"For sixteen years, I've seen Pablo Muñoz's amazing leadership skills firsthand in his work as superintendent of the Elizabeth and Passaic Public Schools. In The Leader's Algorithm, *Pablo shows how he used a personal Theory of Action to transform these highly diverse school systems and improve the lives of his students. For current and aspiring leaders, this book provides a new approach to thinking, working, and leading."*

—DAVID SCIARRA, EXECUTIVE DIRECTOR, EDUCATION LAW CENTER

"I have learned as much about educational leadership from Pablo as I have from anyone. His story is compelling, and his insights and resources are essential for anyone who wants to be a school or district leader. He shows how to make student learning the center of systemic transformation."

—THOMAS HATCH, PROFESSOR, TEACHERS COLLEGE, COLUMBIA UNIVERSITY; DIRECTOR, NATIONAL CENTER FOR RESTRUCTURING EDUCATION, SCHOOLS, AND TEACHING (NCREST); AUTHOR OF *THE EDUCATION WE NEED FOR A FUTURE WE CAN'T PREDICT*

"Pablo Muñoz, one of New Jersey's foremost educational innovators, has authored a pragmatic and inspirational model for leadership that works for executives in education and industry. Practical, effective, and proven."

—GARY S. STEIN, FORMER JUSTICE, NEW JERSEY SUPREME COURT; SPECIAL COUNSEL TO PASHMAN STEIN WALDER HAYDEN

"I always wondered how Pablo Muñoz exhibited such steadfast, courageous, and principled leadership during such complex and challenging circumstances. Now I know. *The Leader's Algorithm* is a must-read for leaders who have both bold visions for change and choppy waters they must navigate in order to get there."

—JOEL ROSE, CO-FOUNDER AND CHIEF EXECUTIVE OFFICER, NEW CLASSROOMS

"*The Leader's Algorithm* is simply exceptional, not only because of its golden content but because of the messenger as well. Pablo is quiet and unassuming, but in this book, he so eloquently expresses his emotions and is so transparent with his struggles, which to me, takes the prize. Success and failure, struggles and triumphs are part of the same package, and Pablo has successfully mixed them all to make this book a great recipe for a life of purpose and for everyone to develop their own Theory of Action for life!"

—RAÚL BURGOS, PRESIDENT, DOMINICANA SE TRANSFORMA

"I watched in real time as Pablo Muñoz transformed the Elizabeth school system from a failing district into a high-performing powerhouse. This is how he did it."

—JAMES COYLE, PRESIDENT, GATEWAY REGIONAL CHAMBER OF COMMERCE

"Pablo's leadership inspired me and countless others to act courageously so that the students in our nation's public schools can thrive. Here, he shares his journey in a compellingly personal way, providing insights to all leaders who strive to make the world a better place."

—DR. BRIAN G. OSBORNE, PROFESSOR OF PRACTICE, LEHIGH UNIVERSITY

"Pablo Muñoz was at the heart of making the Elizabeth Public Schools the best performing by far of New Jersey's major urban districts. There is nothing simple or easy about such an achievement."

—GORDON MACINNES, AUTHOR OF *IN PLAIN SIGHT: SIMPLE, DIFFICULT LESSONS FROM NEW JERSEY'S EXPENSIVE EFFORT TO CLOSE THE ACHIEVEMENT GAP*

THE LEADER'S ALGORITHM

THE LEADER'S ALGORITHM

How a Personal
Theory of Action
Transforms Your Life,
Work, and Relationships

PABLO MUÑOZ

LIONCREST
PUBLISHING

COPYRIGHT © 2023 PABLO MUÑOZ
All rights reserved.

THE LEADER'S ALGORITHM
How a Personal Theory of Action Transforms Your Life, Work, and Relationships

FIRST EDITION

ISBN 978-1-5445-3327-8 *Hardcover*
 978-1-5445-3328-5 *Paperback*
 978-1-5445-3329-2 *Ebook*

To Mami and Papi, thank you for your unconditional love.

To Cecilia and Sadie, I love you unconditionally, too.

CONTENTS

FOREWORD 13

INTRODUCTION 17

1. DEFINING THE LEADER'S ALGORITHM 25

2. LEADING THROUGH VISION 41

3. LEADING THROUGH EXPECTATIONS 59

4. LEADING THROUGH TEAMWORK 83

5. LEADING WITH SKILLS 97

6. LEADING IN YOUR COMMUNITY 117

7. LEADING WITH RESILIENCE 143

8. LEADING WITH LOVE 157

CONCLUSION 167

ACKNOWLEDGMENTS 171

APPENDIX A: PERSONAL THEORIES OF ACTION 175

APPENDIX B: EXAMPLES OF CORPORATE VISION
AND MISSION STATEMENTS 181

APPENDIX C: EXCERPT FROM CAFR FOR ELIZABETH
PUBLIC SCHOOLS, 2012 185

APPENDIX D: DATA DASHBOARDS 203

APPENDIX E: SUPERINTENDENT'S PLAN OF ENTRY—PASSAIC
PUBLIC SCHOOLS, 2013 211

FOREWORD

TIM QUINN, PHD
Founding Managing Director, The Broad Academy
President Emeritus, Northwestern Michigan College
Former Superintendent, Green Bay Public Schools

I first met Pablo Muñoz in 2005 when I interviewed him as a prospective Fellow for The Broad Academy, an intensive elite preparation program for aspiring urban school superintendents. Each year, fifteen to twenty fellows were selected, and, as managing director of that program for almost ten years, I had the opportunity to interview well over five hundred candidates. I was immediately impressed by the strength of Pablo's personal story as the child of first-generation immigrants, and his remarkable journey to educational leadership.

During the course of the yearlong academy, I got to know Pablo well, and considered him one of the more *thoughtful* learners we'd had in any of our cohorts. Then, as a colleague and coach over the succeeding fifteen years, I have had a "ringside seat" to his career, observing as he successfully tackled the challenges of two urban superintendencies.

As superintendent, he was masterful at connecting his personal values, learning, and growth with the needs and then the performance of the two school systems he led. As a highly intelligent and reflective person by nature, he was able to develop and articulate effective strategies for success. Under his tireless leadership, the districts raised achievement and closed achievement gaps between children of wealth and children of poverty. Unlike many urban superintendents, he not only carefully and thoughtfully considered what needed to be done, but he survived long enough in the roles to have a lasting impact on the culture and performance of the districts he led.

Pablo is not a person to seek recognition and public accolades for himself, although his performance certainly deserved celebration. That is why I'm glad that upon his "retirement" from the superintendency he has taken the opportunity to write this book highlighting his learning and experiences that will provide incredibly valuable guidance for other leaders.

Through this book—by sharing his journey, his values, his beliefs, and his personal Theory of Action—Pablo demonstrates what leaders can accomplish when they take the time to think and reflect on the things that really make a difference for the children being served. By clearly understanding and articulating who they are, what their life is about, what they believe success to be (on a personal and organizational level), and what they believe will lead to that success, amazing results can occur.

Pablo was one of the too-few superintendents in America who not only enjoyed the position, but who embraced and relished the hard work of teaching and learning. His legacy and his methods are a model for school leaders everywhere. He is among the very best that I have known.

INTRODUCTION

"...heed the discipline of your father, and do not forsake the instruction of your mother..."

—PROVERBS 1:8

My first memories of school are sparse but vivid: kindergarten in my hometown of Elizabeth, New Jersey. My *Adam-12* lunchbox, covered in action shots of police officers and patrol cars. Inside, there were ham-and-cheese sandwiches wrapped in foil, so that by lunchtime the cheese was half-melted and delicious. I can still almost taste the Welch's grape juice, served in a little can with a pull tab. I remember the horror of having to *hold hands* with my field-trip buddy, and the fun of playing with trucks and blocks.

But my most visceral—and painful—memory of kindergarten isn't about food or friends. It's about leadership and expectations.

The classroom had a small coatroom area with cubbies. One day after class, my teacher pulled my mother aside in the coatroom and scolded her because I didn't know my colors yet. Her voice was cold and harsh, and she warned my mother that I would be held back unless I learned them. The words hung in the air until my mom began to cry. I hugged her leg and cried, too.

I felt that it was bitterly unfair. I knew my colors just fine—in Spanish. I just didn't know them in English. My teacher either wasn't aware of that, or she didn't care. She didn't take the time to have a real conversation with my mom, or to discover that she couldn't read or write in English yet either.

The teacher didn't offer to work with me or show my mother any picture books that might help. She just shamed us and predicted failure. My mom and I cried together, because we didn't know that the real failure here was a failure of leadership. Instead of setting an expectation that would lift me up, that teacher tore me down.

ELEVATING LEADERSHIP

In the years since, especially my thirty years as a teacher and school administrator, I've learned that good leadership is essential to good education. In order for the teachers to lead well, they must be led well. That leadership starts from the top: the district superintendent.

Many current and aspiring superintendents don't really understand what the job entails, and don't know how to do it. I know, because I felt the same way. I was fortunate to have great advocates and mentors who invested in me personally, but my main models for leadership development were books. I hope this book can help you in turn. The struggle of learning on the job is incredibly stressful.

The gaps in a superintendent's skillset, and more importantly, the gaps in their understanding of leadership, create a culture of low expectations and underperformance. Such a culture will permeate the whole school system and ultimately undermine the best intentions and best efforts of every administrator, supervisor, and classroom teacher. Our schools and our communities need great superintendents!

Systems of all kinds resist change. That's true whether you're talking about natural systems, family systems, social systems, business systems, or school systems. Once an underperforming culture takes hold in a district, it will perpetuate itself until someone steps up (or steps in) to change it. Effective leaders solve problems, and when there are systemic problems, leaders must make systemic changes.

That's my vision for writing this book: to share my learning from a long career as a changemaker in educational leadership. Much of that learning was done in the trenches, but I have also gleaned a great deal of knowledge from leadership principles and materials targeted to the business world. Those big-picture insights about human nature and team development don't usually get translated into formal training for educators. I hope this book will fill that gap.

In these pages, you'll learn how to develop and apply a framework I call the Leader's Algorithm. The Leader's Algorithm integrates your personal and professional goals with your organization's vision and mission, to generate a clear and compelling personal Theory of Action. When you execute that theory with direct, consistent steps, and make yourself accountable for the outcome, you can transform your life, work, and relationships.

Throughout the book, I'll share key leadership principles, along with real-world situations that helped me learn each principle and put it into practice. We'll start with setting a vision and mission that can elevate your organization. We'll examine how high expectations can inspire team members and students to unprecedented achievement. I'll discuss how to build a strong team and empower them to deliver excellent results, as well as how to help your team develop the skills they need.

Beyond your team, we'll look at ways you can become a leader in your community, so that your stakeholders understand and support your vision. We'll address some of the challenges and stresses that come with leadership, to help you cultivate personal resilience and a network of support. Above all, you'll learn to lead from the heart, because great leadership is an act of love.

LEARNING TO LEAD

Leadership through love has always inspired and sustained me. Despite the inauspicious beginnings of my academic career in that kindergarten coatroom, I was blessed with parents who believed in me and saw my true potential. My mom was certain that I could do anything I set my mind to, and certainly wasn't going to let me flunk kindergarten. Not only did I learn my colors, I became a first-generation high school graduate and went on to earn a bachelor's degree from Yale University and a master's from Columbia University.

At the same time, my father devoted himself to teaching me baseball. His long hours practicing with me and advocating for me got me onto championship teams. Those early experiences in youth leagues led to collegiate ball, and eventually to coaching for a Major League Baseball club. As a player and a coach, I absorbed important lessons about teamwork, mentoring, and leading through excellence.

Those lessons informed my work when I returned to the Elizabeth Public Schools as a teacher. The desire to create an environment of excellence propelled me to become the director of curriculum and instruction, then assistant superintendent, and in 2005, superintendent of schools.

Elizabeth Public Schools is one of the largest districts in New Jersey, and one of the most deeply disadvantaged—at the time, approximately 86 percent of the student body qualified for free or reduced-price meals. Historically, it was designated as an "Abbott district," in reference to a court finding that the inequality between the state's richest and poorest schools was unconstitutionally depriving students of educational opportunity. My directive—and my personal goal—was to provide students with an education just as rigorous and valuable as the wealthiest districts in the state, or even the country.

Education is a powerful lever for individual students and for whole communities. It allows students to move from poverty to wealth, to have meaningful choices in their work and for their families. It allows them to achieve the American dream. Lifting a school district's performance can break generational cycles of poverty and deprivation. I knew going into the job that leading the district to excellence had the potential to change thousands of lives.

In the eight and a half years of my tenure as superintendent in Elizabeth, I began learning and practicing the elements that would become my Leader's Algorithm. That approach helped me and my team transform the district from one of the worst to one of the best. We received three National Blue Ribbon awards from the US Department of Education, and two of our high schools rose to top rankings for the state, as well as to national indexes like *US News & World Report*, *Newsweek*, and the *Washington Post*.

In 2013, I transitioned to the Passaic Public Schools. Though the challenges were different, it was still an underperforming urban school district with over 88 percent of students being economically disadvantaged. The lessons learned in Elizabeth formed a strong foundation, but Passaic's needs required me to continue growing and learning. I was in an iterative process of refining my Leader's Algorithm, though I hadn't named it yet.

Applying my Leader's Algorithm during my seven and a half years as superintendent in Passaic created life-changing results for our students. We created an immersive bilingual program for elementary students that was designated as a model program for the state. We achieved double-digit (and in a few grades, triple-digit) increases in student proficiency in math and English. In order to promote all students' readiness for college or high-paying careers, we created dual-enrollment pathways for students to graduate high school with transferable college credits or an associate's degree. We also created three specialized high schools: college prep, STEM-focused, and a school for career and technical programs.

TRANSFORMING YOURSELF

The turnarounds in those school districts were complex, large-scale undertakings that required time to implement. The work is ongoing, and it never stops. I'm not going to offer a prescriptive manual or step-by-step formula for running a school district. There isn't one. I also have no intention of creating an exposé on local issues in my districts.

Instead, I offer you a guide to personal development that will help you embrace the philosophy of leadership. I hope this book will help you form a leadership style that serves your organization, your team, your students, and yourself in a holistic and transformative way. The first step of that process is to ask yourself one vital question: what kind of growth and transformation do you seek? This is the beginning of your Leader's Algorithm.

CHAPTER 1

DEFINING THE LEADER'S ALGORITHM

"Discipline is the bridge between goals and accomplishment."

—MOTHER TERESA

My high school baseball coach Ray Korn taught me how to pitch, and how to lead.

Now, don't get me wrong: my father was my first baseball coach. He had a ball and glove in my hand by the time I was three years old. He showed me how to throw, catch, hit, and run the bases. He drilled me on fundamentals until I could compete at a high level, and advocated to get me into Little League. He pushed me, drove me hard, and poured his love and attention into me because he believed in me. He gave me a powerful model of leadership through action and relationships.

But when I got onto Coach Korn's team at Elizabeth High School, he instructed me in technique. He broke down the mechanics of pitching. He taught me how to approach hitters. He taught me to think strategically about pitching, and gave me the specific skills to carry out those strategies in different situations. That strategic thinking transformed me into a pitcher, later from a pitcher to a pitching coach, and then stayed with me as a teacher, administrator, and superintendent.

Strategic thinking is the difference between playing *in* a game and playing *the* game: being a participant or being a leader. In the same way, the Leader's Algorithm depends on thoughtful deliberation of your desired outcome, and strategic choices of what actions will achieve those goals.

The Leader's Algorithm is an equation that puts strategic thinking to work: your personal Theory of Action, executed consistently with public accountability, will transform your life, work, and relationships. It is a recipe for success.

THE LEADER'S ALGORITHM:

Personal TOA + Execution + Accountability = Transformation

In order to understand this equation, let's look first at what a Theory of Action is and how it works. In this chapter, we'll see the difference between organizational and personal Theories of Action. We'll discuss the importance of consistent execution and accountability in order to accomplish your own transformation as a leader. Finally, I'll show you how to compose a personal Theory of Action for yourself.

WHAT IS A THEORY OF ACTION?

A Theory of Action (TOA) is a widely used tool, and if you've done formal study in educational leadership you've probably encountered it many times. You may even have created them for yourself. Whether you have or not, let me take a moment to discuss this concept so we can approach it from the same perspective.

A TOA is a hypothesis that certain actions will lead to certain results. For a school district, an organizational TOA is a logical sequence of values, intentions, and actions that will lead to defined goals. It provides a clear framework for developing strategic plans, identifying priorities, and setting milestone targets. Once those are in place, the path forward and any necessary actions you'll need to take are clearly defined. In simplest terms, a TOA is a roadmap of what the organization needs to do to accomplish its mission. Organizational TOAs are usually reflected in policy statements, and become a directive to management to make personnel, budget, and program decisions based on these overarching concepts. You'll find an in-depth examination of organizational TOAs in *What School Boards Can Do: Reform Governance for Urban Schools*.[1]

The power of an organizational TOA—and what makes it different from an ordinary list of goals or a mission statement—is that it requires you to think strategically about specific steps the organization needs to take to realize its vision. It is a statement of belief about the system itself and the way to effect change. It is both philosophical and practical.

---

[1] Donald R. McAdams. *What School Boards Can Do: Reform Governance for Urban Schools*, New York, NY: Teachers College Press, 2006.

MAKE IT PERSONAL

An organizational TOA comes from the school board or a governing body. A personal Theory of Action comes from you, the individual leader. I first learned the concept through my work with the New Jersey Network of Superintendents and the book *Instructional Rounds in Education: A Network Approach to Improving Teaching and Learning*.[2] In its original form, a personal Theory of Action is presented as a simple one- or two-sentence statement to help solve a problem of practice. In the Leader's Algorithm, I've created an expanded personal TOA that is a broader plan of how to operate as a leader.

To create this expanded type of personal TOA as part of your Leader's Algorithm, you take the organizational goals and milestones and make a hypothesis about what you can do personally and through your team to get where you are all trying to go. While an organizational TOA is expressed as declarative statements about what the district will do, a personal TOA lays out a logical chain of *if-then* statements that lead to your desired outcome. Your personal TOA becomes a leadership statement that reflects your beliefs about people and relationships as well as the system they're operating in. It articulates your definition of an effective leader.

Without a personal TOA, your thoughts and actions become unfocused. You can easily be knocked off course by changes in circumstance or influence from others. You may become reactive and lose sight of your long-term goals, or you may be distracted by new opportunities and waste time and resources pursuing programs that don't advance your core mission. The

---

[2] Elizabeth A. City, Richard F. Elmore, Sarah E. Fiarman, and Lee Teitel. *Instructional Rounds in Education: A Network Approach to Improving Teaching and Learning*, Cambridge, MA: Harvard Education Press, 2009.

logical flow of "*if* I do this, *then* that will be the outcome" keeps your end goal constantly in view.

In a personal TOA that you design for your individual work or your private life, each step in the chain of causality would be an action that you can execute on your own. But as a leader, you don't work in isolation. Leadership is getting results with and through people, so your personal TOA for a leadership role involves a chain of causality that branches out like a Christmas tree. Your actions ignite actions from others that spread out through your organization and affect the whole system.

In my personal Theories of Action, I've always looked at the people on my management team who will help me carry out my personal TOA. Who are they? What qualities should I look for in choosing those team members? What do they need to do? Then, as I move down the steps of the personal TOA, I branch out to system-wide actions that will ultimately effect change for every one of our students.

For example, in Elizabeth Public Schools, I hypothesized that:

- *If* I led with focus on vision and mission, selected effective leaders, and got resources into the classrooms;
- *If* those leaders focused on the right areas;
- *If* we got the whole system committed to Managed Instruction;[3] and
- *If* the whole system committed to certain guiding principles;

Then our students would think, learn, achieve, and care—which would result in our students being prepared to pursue a college education and high-paying jobs.

Each of those top-level *if* statements breaks down into more detailed, specific steps, and you can read the whole statement in Appendix A at the back of the book. For now, I want you to see the way that these premises cascade down from the leader, through the management team, out to the district and the students. The leader's strategic choices create a path for the team and the system to follow. Indeed, "think, learn, achieve, and care" became a slogan for the district and part of our brand.

CONSISTENT EXECUTION

When you're creating your personal TOA, you're putting thought into how you're going to lead and what variables are

---

[3] Donald R. McAdams. *What School Boards Can Do: Reform Governance for Urban Schools*, New York, NY: Teachers College Press, 2006.

most important to get you to your goals. Then you have to be disciplined enough to do all the work that you laid out in those "if" statements.

In *The Art of War*, Sun Tzu said, "Every battle is won before it is ever fought."[4] I learned this principle on the ballfield instead of the battlefield—that the game is won before you play the game. It speaks to the importance of preparation and consistency. In sports, if you practice well and do enough repetitions, you'll create muscle memory so that your body performs the right actions without you having to think about it in the moment. That's crucial, because in the game—the moment of execution—there's no time to get ready. You have to walk in ready.

The same holds true in executing the components of your personal Theory of Action. The actions you'll include in your personal TOA aren't one-time efforts, like making an announcement or purchasing a piece of equipment. They are long-term patterns of thought, behavior, and communication. You will execute those actions over and over, every month, every week, and every day. In time, they become reflexes—you, your team, and your organization will be prepared to respond consistently, even in unpredictable situations.

You must be disciplined enough to stick with your strategy, but flexible enough to realize when something is not working. The first draft of your personal TOA may not be calibrated quite right for your district's unique circumstances, particularly if you're entering a new role or a new district. Your Leader's Algorithm must adapt to the context in which you're working.

---

[4] Sun Tzu, *The Art of War*, Chichester, England: Capstone Publishing, 2010.

TESTING AND ADJUSTING

As with any hypothesis, your Leader's Algorithm needs to be tested in the real world. You must turn your *if* statements into actions to see the results. The author Warren Bennis once said that "leadership is the capacity to translate vision into reality." In the same way, your personal Theory of Action can't remain a theory. It must be put into practice.

As you do so, you can assess whether the actions are working to achieve your ultimate goal, your *then*. Failing to achieve your goals is part of the feedback loop. That failure is a signal that you need to make an adjustment. Perhaps your *if* statements are not correct. Perhaps you didn't really follow through on preparation. Perhaps your personal blind spots created weak spots in your logical sequence.

That was sometimes the case for me. I had a very clear vision of what I wanted to accomplish for the students, and I focused intently on getting the students prepared academically to go off to college and have great careers. However, sometimes I was less focused on social and emotional learning for the kids. Sometimes I was less focused on building relationships with key stakeholders that could make or break initiatives. Those failings forced me to reevaluate and revise my personal TOA so it would better reflect the full scope of what we were trying to achieve, and serve as a better roadmap to those outcomes.

Failure is a lesson, not an ending. You don't quit. You have to make a shift, get up, and go again. You start over in a different way.

PUBLIC ACCOUNTABILITY

Your thoughts are mental models of how you want to lead. It's important for you to put them in writing and share them publicly. Making your personal TOA public is beneficial to your management team and your organization in many different ways. First, it enhances your relationship with your team—they need to know who you are, what you believe, what you intend to accomplish, and how you will go about it. That relationship is the basis of your influence with the leaders operating under you. When they understand your values and beliefs, they can trust you and feel confident about where the organization is going.

Next, sharing your personal TOA gives your management team a set of guiding principles to act on. By following the logic of your personal TOA, they can act in alignment with your goals and values as they make independent decisions in their own areas of responsibility.

Making your personal TOA public also helps district stakeholders discuss and articulate the district's own values, goals, and beliefs. Most school districts have some kind of vision or mission statement, and they probably have some kind of unspoken Theory of Action in effect. After all, everyone has some kind of belief system about the way leadership works. They make choices because they believe it will lead to some desired result. But most school districts don't deal with policy from a theoretical perspective, so there is no cohesive organizational TOA statement that memorializes those guiding principles. Each person operates on their individual set of beliefs—which may contradict each other or lead them away from your goals. When a superintendent shares a clear, logical personal TOA, this transparency helps break down silos and align all the stakeholders so they can cooperate more effectively.

Finally, sharing your personal TOA makes you publicly accountable to your board, your students, the parents, and your community. Sharing invites stakeholders to weigh in with their own beliefs about the way the system works. That can be valuable insight into your district! If you or your team are not acting in alignment with your personal TOA, your stakeholders have the right to question you about it. They can compare your real results with your stated goals and see the progress you're making. All this transparency increases trust and cooperation at every level in your district, which will maximize your influence and ability to make change.

In his book *The 21 Indispensable Qualities of a Leader,* John Maxwell said, "Everything rises and falls on leadership."[5] In that statement, he is referring not to the leader's techniques, but to their character qualities. I've seen that to be true in athletics, in schools, and in districts—ineffective leadership will produce ineffective organizations. Effective leaders with big and bold visions can create excellent results and, given time, can create outcomes that many would have thought impossible. When your personal TOA is a public document, the public can set high expectations for you and challenge you to be your best self as a leader.

YOUR TURN

Now I want to show you how to write your personal Theory of Action, using the template page at the end of this chapter. I'll

---

[5] John C. Maxwell, *The 21 Indispensable Qualities of a Leader: Becoming the Person Others Will Want to Follow,* Nashville: Nelson Books, 1999, p XI.

draw on examples from my own personal TOAs in the Elizabeth and Passaic districts, and you can find the full text of both documents in Appendix A. I'll note that my experience and examples are from the point of view of a superintendent or senior executive. These principles also apply to those who are leading change from other positions within an organization. I encourage you to take these principles and extrapolate them to your own situation.

The first step is to define your ultimate goal. Remember, the impact of the leader's choices flows down from the top, but in order to create a viable personal TOA, the leader must start with the bottom line by crafting the right goals.

In Elizabeth Public Schools, my ultimate goal was *for our students to graduate prepared to pursue a college education; to think, learn, achieve, and care; and to receive high pay in the 21st century marketplace.*

In Passaic Public Schools, my goal was very similar: *to create a top-tier school system that prepared our students to attend college and to earn high pay in the 21st century marketplace.*

Those were the most important changes I could make in underperforming school systems in highly disadvantaged communities. If you will be leading in a district where college and career success are taken for granted, academic improvement may not be the biggest need for you to address. Perhaps your students have pressing social and emotional needs. Perhaps your community needs a vibrant sense of citizenship, civic duty, and public service. Perhaps your school district needs to address equity. Whatever those needs may be, your ultimate goal should be an inflection point that will make lasting positive change in the lives of your students and their families. Take some time to consider those needs and the best outcome that would meet them.

What is your ultimate goal?

Now, consider the guiding principles that will shape your choices and help your management team keep their decisions and actions in alignment with the same set of core values. Consider your personal values and beliefs about what will move people toward the ultimate goal, as well as the stated values of the organization.

Don't overcomplicate this step—two or three principles are enough. I find that branding these values makes complex concepts easier to digest and repeat so that staff, students, and parents can remember and act on them. For example, in Elizabeth our core values were known as the **3 Ls**:

- Love,
- Laser-like focus on teaching and learning, and
- Leadership.

In Passaic, we used the **2 Qs** as our guiding principles:

- **Quantity** (more instructional time and access to learning opportunities) and
- **Quality** (frequent and meaningful feedback and professional development to make teaching and leading more effective).

What guiding principles will help the whole district move together toward the ultimate goal?

Next, we need to identify a concrete objective that will create significant leverage toward your ultimate goal. This objective will dictate a number of specific actions for you and your team to execute. For example, my objectives in both school districts were to *systematically improve instruction*. Those objectives generated action steps around curriculum development, workforce recruitment and retention, professional development, assessments and interventions, and performance measurement. You may already have a specific objective in mind that would form a major milestone toward your ultimate goal. If so, consider what actions will make that objective a reality.

What objective will you move the district toward? What action steps will achieve this objective?

You can't achieve objectives on your own. You need to identify and develop leaders within the organization who will move the district forward with clear focus on the right priorities. Consider the values and beliefs that they demonstrate in their work, as well as their character as leaders. What areas of focus will make leadership the most effective in achieving your objective and your ultimate goal? You can use any number that works for you, but I wouldn't advise adding much more than six. Trying to focus on too many things isn't focus. It's distraction.

The common themes in both my districts were that I selected

leaders who focused on *vision and mission, improving the instructional core, teamwork, and trust.*

What should your management team focus on?

Now that you have a clear map of where you are trying to go, it's time to decide your own focus as a leader. I recommend that you limit yourself to three priorities that will have the most impact. This is your strongest statement of belief about what an effective superintendent should do.

I used the same three actions in both districts, because ultimately I believe this is the clearest way to state the superintendent's job:

- Keep the school system focused on its vision and mission in an effort to produce excellent results,
- Select effective leaders to carry out the mission, and
- Get the resources into the classroom.

What actions can you take to move your district from its current state to your ultimate goal?

When you know your answers to these questions, you can construct your personal TOA:

If I lead with a focus on…

If I select leaders who focus on…

If I move the district toward this objective…

If I develop the school system through these guiding principles…

Then we will…

As you contemplate your answers to all these elements of the personal TOA, take your time and make as many drafts as you need to. These beliefs, priorities, and actions will need to be refined as you gain insight about your district, about your team, and about yourself as a leader. Make sure that you have spent time listening and learning to the administrators, teachers, parents, and other stakeholders in your district so that your personal TOA thoughtfully addresses real strengths and weaknesses in your organization, as well as the needs and concerns of the community. You will make this document public, but before you do, make sure it is as strong and clear as it can be.

Your ultimate goal, your guiding principles, and the right areas for your management team to focus on are all guided by the vision and mission of your organization. Your influence and effectiveness as a leader are rooted in your ability to understand and articulate this vision and mission and instill it in others. That's what we'll address in the next chapter, "Leading through Vision."

PERSONAL THEORY OF ACTION TEMPLATE

<YOUR ORGANIZATION NAME>

<your name>
<your job title>

MY THEORY OF ACTION

<date>

If I lead with a focus on:

1.
2.
3.

If I select leaders who focus on:

1.
2.
3.
(or more)

If I move the district toward this objective:

1.

If I develop the school system through these guiding principles:

1.
2.
3.

Then we will…

CHAPTER 2

LEADING THROUGH VISION

"Dare to live the life you have dreamed for yourself. Go forward and make your dreams come true."

—RALPH WALDO EMERSON

When I was an assistant superintendent in Elizabeth, one of the schools I oversaw was Elizabeth High School. It was a large, sprawling school with five thousand students spread over several different buildings. The day-to-day operations of each building, or "house," were run by house directors, who were each certified as principals and functioned on the same level as school principals for their house. The principal of the whole high school functioned on a similar level to an assistant superintendent. It was a huge operation.

I was assigned to give the principal his annual evaluation. Now, this principal was a good manager. There was good order and student discipline. The trains ran on time, you might say. I gave him good ratings on all those categories and paid him compliments on his effectiveness in those areas. Then, I addressed the academics at the school. They weren't good. I encouraged him to put more effort into improving teaching and learning.

That didn't go well. We had both worked in the district for a long time, and we'd had a contentious relationship in the past. He really didn't appreciate the way I was pushing him on improving instruction. He was the principal of the largest school in the district, possibly in the state, and in his mind he was doing very well at an extremely challenging job.

Not long after that, I got a call from the district superintendent. He said that the principal told him I was "bothering him."

I didn't know what he was talking about, but since the last time I'd spoken to the principal was during the evaluation, I suspected it might be that exchange. I explained that I'd given a routine evaluation, pointed out all the things he was doing well, and addressed the items that needed improvement. That's what you do in an evaluation.

At that point, the superintendent said, in effect, "Pablo, I need you to leave him alone. He's doing a good job keeping that school in line. If the lid comes off that school, there's five thousand kids. Holy hell's going to break loose and it'll be chaos. This guy is keeping a lid on it, and I need him to do that."

The superintendent was also a good manager and an excellent politician—he'd even been a state Superintendent of the Year. But I realized at that moment that we would never see eye to eye. He was very demanding of his staff, but had no real aspirations for the students. He was invested in perpetuating a system that was just *functional*, nothing more. He wanted to manage well, but never discussed vision or mission. I wanted to create an excellent school system that would forever change our students' lives for the better, and I had a vision of what was possible to achieve.

This situation perfectly illustrates the difference between management and leadership. Both the superintendent and the principal were effective administrators, but they were lacking in leadership, because they lacked vision. As a leader, you set the culture, expectations, and direction of the organization. Your team, your staff, and your students will rise (or sink) to match your expectations. Remember, all significant accomplishments in history have been achieved by aiming high, not aiming low.

In fact, focusing on academic excellence doesn't take away from order or discipline. It makes it easier to keep order. Students are smart human beings. Whether they are in kindergarten or in high school, with high academics or low, they are smart. They lack life experience, but they know when you care about them. They can see the reasons behind your rules and regulations, your grading policies, your attendance policies, your rigorous courses, excellent teaching, challenging homework, and project assignments. They can see that you ask more from them because you care, and *you believe they are capable.*

Students who are being challenged may complain. They don't necessarily enjoy it. Sometimes they get frustrated, especially when they don't yet have the proficiency to hit the standards you set. But when students are busy with their studies and focused on improving their skills, they're less interested in acting out and being undisciplined.

There will always be some percentage of students who refuse to come on board with your high expectations. Behavior problems will never magically disappear, but individual behavior problems don't become widespread if the majority of the students are engaged. When the students are not belittled by your expectations and the way those expectations manifest in your policies and assignments, they feel respected. They are more likely to return that respect. You keep the critical mass of students pursuing excellence, and you won't need to "keep a lid on it." You can blow the lid of low expectations right off the top.

This superintendent and principal didn't have a vision for the district beyond maintaining the status quo. Without a clear and compelling vision, they had lost touch with the district's real purpose: educating students. As King Solomon said in Proverbs 29:18, "Where there is no vision, the people perish." The students' potential was perishing because their administrators had no vision for their future.

"Where there is no vision, the people perish."

—PROVERBS 29:18

VISION COMES FIRST

The ultimate goal articulated in your Leader's Algorithm is an expression of your vision. Vision and mission are often used interchangeably or considered as a single unit. However, they are distinct concepts, and you need to be able to articulate both vision and mission for your organization. Your vision is what you want the organization to be in the future. By focusing on the future, you are always pursuing change and improvement. You're leading people to focus on how they can make things better, not just telling them to keep their heads above water.

At the same time, your vision gives the organization a single, clear direction to follow. Without it, there's no focus—everyone wants to go somewhere, anywhere, and any destination would be fine. Everyone has their own interpretation of what it means to make progress, so nobody is pulling in the same direction. You become paralyzed and stagnant.

In order to engage and motivate people, your vision must be relevant and believable for your organization. For a school district, relevance means that your vision is tied to improving academic performance, improving the way the district serves students, and giving the students more and better options in their future lives. Believability means that the vision can be accomplished in a reasonable time frame, not someday in the misty future. While you want to set big goals, you also want to make sure that your teachers, administrators, and stakeholders can take the vision seriously and have confidence in working toward it.

In a best-case scenario, you would achieve your vision in a few years and then update it so that the organization keeps moving forward. In Elizabeth, when I started out, we set a vision to become one of the best school districts in New Jersey. Five years out, after making significant academic progress, we achieved that. We updated the vision statement to become one of the best school districts in the United States. My plan for the next step was to set a vision that we would become one of the best in the world. I always set out my vision five years at a time, because those were standard contract terms.

When I transitioned to Passaic, the context was very different. At the time, the district was in the bottom 50 percent for academic performance among Abbott school districts, and even lower in statewide rankings. They received the same funding as all the other comparable districts, but still had structure problems, talent-development problems, management problems, and leadership problems. I didn't think the organization was ready to believe that we could be the best in the country or the best in the state. Instead, I set a vision that we would become one of the best *urban* school districts in the state, which would put us on par with an average New Jersey district. I felt that was doable, and that all my stakeholders could buy into that vision without experiencing cognitive dissonance or feeling overwhelmed.

Your vision must be a living document that begins where you are right now and points the organization in the direction you want to go. A strong, simple vision will generate a compelling mission and concrete actions to put that mission into practice.

Vision is what you want the organization to be in the future.

MISSION EXECUTES VISION

The next step you take toward the ultimate goal in your Leader's Algorithm is the expression of your mission. Your mission is what you do every day when you come to work. It is how you make your vision come to life. For example, in Passaic our mission statement was that we would provide an excellent education that prepares students for college and high-paying jobs.

There are two parts to that mission statement: what the adults do and what the students do. The teachers, administrators, board, and parents work together to provide an excellent education and great opportunities for the students. The students work hard so they are prepared to take advantage of those opportunities, and so they will have the same quality and quantity of options as any of their peers in affluent communities.

Now, we're all human. We will all have days when we don't execute our mission perfectly. When that happens, we don't lower our expectations or give up on the mission. We get up the next day, look in the mirror, and go back to work. We start over in our commitment to carrying out our mission.

Mission is what we do every day to bring our vision to life.

WRITE IT, SPEAK IT, WALK IT

Many districts have a stated vision and mission that originated from the board or a committee. Rarely are those statements living, purposeful messages that truly guide and inspire the staff and students. Often, if you ask a teacher or administrator about the district's vision, they couldn't even tell you what it is. I recall seeing a cartoon some years ago that depicted a group of people at a conference table and a character standing at a flip chart with nothing written on it but the letter "I." The caption read, "A sentence written by committee." Every time I hear about a vision or mission statement written by a committee, I get a chuckle.

I believe that the strongest vision comes from an individual leader—the superintendent. Naturally it needs to be vetted, refined, and adopted by your stakeholders. That's part of the process of getting buy-in from everyone involved. But as the leader, you should spearhead the formation and promotion of the vision.

When it comes to gaining buy-in (as with every other aspect of leadership), context matters. A private-sector business is accountable to owners or shareholders. A school district is owned by the community it serves, and in the public school system many factors affect the context of your leadership—whether the district is urban, suburban, or rural; whether the school board is elected or appointed by the mayor, and so forth. All these factors impact a leader's approach.

A superintendent has many constraints: laws, rules, policies, the desires of the board and other elected officials—but in the end, you control what you write, say, and do. When I went through the hiring process, I was clear with the board about my commitment to a vision and mission for the district, and the direction I intended to take. We had alignment on the major ideas from the start, because I was hired to improve teaching and learning. This was particularly true in Elizabeth, because nobody in the district was talking about vision or mission at all. There was a vacuum ready for me to step into. I took my direction from my "book mentors" Jack Welch, John Maxwell, and Roberto Goizueta, who all emphasize that it's the leader's responsibility to be clear about vision and mission.

Your stakeholders can provide valuable insight to hone your vision and mission. Listening to their feedback helps you build relationships and ensure that they feel included. We'll talk more about influence and persuasion with stakeholders in Chapter Six. For now, I want you to understand that you will be the one writing, speaking, and acting on the vision and mission—so the final responsibility lies with you.

Some people write paragraphs of flowery prose to describe their vision. If you need to work through that as part of your thought process, go right ahead. But don't hold onto those long, wordy statements when you finalize it. In my experience, overly long and complex vision statements tend to be full of stock phrases that don't have much to do with the real experiences and motivations of the people in the organization. Administrators don't emphasize them. Nobody cares enough to remember them.

Instead, distill the vision down into a single sentence that's easy to repeat, remember, and display. You'll be doing all those things, over and over again. I agree with Jack Welch's approach, that "leaders create a vision, articulate the vision, passionately own the vision and relentlessly drive it to completion." You need to repeat that vision, repeat it again, and keep repeating it until your people live and breathe it. Repeat it until they gag on it, if you have to.

In Elizabeth, I repeated the vision, mission, and the 3 Ls. In Passaic, it was the vision, mission, and our focus: *to provide all students the opportunity to graduate high school with a career certification, a minimum of 15 college credits, or both.* I wanted to be clear within the organization and with the external stakeholders what the school district was trying to accomplish. You need every staff member, teacher, and student in your school district to know, support, and pursue that vision. They need to see it everywhere they look, every day. It needs to be given to them in presentations, in announcements and meetings, in website posts, in posters and hallway displays, on public reports, and everywhere else you can possibly put it forward.

As a matter of fact, I used to begin my meetings with administrators or with my cabinet by calling on people to state our vision, mission, and focus, and I'd recommend that practice to you. That vision needs to become second nature to everyone involved. They need to see their future. They need to know where they are headed, so they can't possibly lose their way.

> In Appendix B, you'll find examples of single-sentence vision statements and mission statements from many different types of corporations, as stated on their company websites or annual reports. In Appendix C, you'll find examples of repeating the vision, mission, and guiding principles in excerpts from the Comprehensive Annual Financial Report (CAFR) for Elizabeth. This report to the board and the community isn't just facts and figures. It's an opportunity to draw a direct line from our vision, mission, and guiding principles, through our major initiatives, to the results we achieved for our students. You can see how every aspect of our work originated from my personal TOA and was expressed through our vision, mission, and guiding principles, from curriculum changes to facility updates. Vision, mission, and guiding principles govern everything you do.

Above all, you need to demonstrate that vision with your own actions and choices. As St. Francis of Assisi said, "There's no use walking anywhere to preach unless our walking is our preaching." People will see whether or not you are acting in alignment with the vision you're promoting. When a leader says one thing with their words but something different with their actions, it's the actions that people follow. Make sure that your actions are backing up your vision statement and following through on your mission.

Write a simple, memorable vision statement. Repeat it constantly. Act on it consistently.

TURNING VISION INTO CULTURE

When you set a big, compelling vision for your district, backed up by a mission that makes it possible, it challenges people. A new vision requires a new culture in your organization to carry it out, and it's normal for there to be resistance to a cultural change. Your board, your parents, or your staff may question your vision or disagree. That's fine! Debate is healthy. If people are asking questions and having strong reactions, that gives you two pieces of good news: First, it means they understand and remember the vision and mission. Second, it means that they are engaged, and the vision and mission are having an impact.

The debates that happened in Passaic about our vision and mission statements were very interesting. On one hand, I was surprised by the number of people who pushed back on the mission statement that we would prepare students for college and high-paying jobs.

Parents would attend board meetings, come up to the microphone, and ask, "What if my kid doesn't want to go to college?" Or "Why does everyone need a high-paying job?" Sometimes high school students would do the same. I had to explain that a good education doesn't limit a student's choices, it expands them. If a student doesn't choose to go to college, nobody is going to force them—but if they aren't prepared for college, that's not a free choice. If a student chooses a career that is more about passion than a paycheck, a good education will help them excel at that career anyway. We don't want students forced into minimum-wage jobs because they aren't prepared to achieve more. The kids in the suburbs take that preparation for granted. In our district, we needed to be intentional about it.

On the other hand, there were board members who didn't think my vision was big enough. I'd set a vision to become the best urban school district in the state, and some members wanted to be the best in all of New Jersey. I agreed with them! I had to explain that we needed to set a vision that everyone could see coming true. When we made it a reality, we could (and would) set a new vision to be the best in the state, or the country. We needed to be strategic about our progression so we could bring everyone along with us.

The fact that we were having these debates in a deeply broken system was fantastic. Despite the problems that needed fixing, everyone cared about where we were trying to go, and how we could get there. Everyone was talking about the students' futures—and that's exactly what a vision statement should do.

A strong vision provokes strong responses.

CHANGING CULTURE

Leading educational improvement is about moving from the current state and culture to a new, desired state and culture. As a general rule, I didn't address culture directly or publicly during my superintendencies. I had some one-on-one or small-group discussions about it, but for the most part I addressed culture through my actions rather than through my words.

In order to change the culture of an organization, you have to change people's beliefs about the work they are doing, their role in the organization, and to a certain extent their beliefs about themselves. You can't do that by simply declaring that everyone must now have a new set of beliefs. It isn't respectful, it isn't intellectually honest, and it simply doesn't work.

Instead, you need to change people's behavior. To do that, you create policies, practices, procedures, and systems. You develop or change personnel. As people act on these new policies and practices, they start to see improvements. They see success. Those new behaviors become self-reinforcing, and with time, people's beliefs change because of what they have seen and experienced for themselves. They become emotionally invested in the new way of doing things, and take ownership of the practices. Those new beliefs, repeated and manifested through changed behavior, create a changed culture.

Changed behavior changes beliefs. Changed beliefs change culture.

CHANGING PERSONNEL

John Maxwell uses an example of leadership and vision that has always stuck with me. He writes that when a sports team brings in a new coach, they don't fire all the players. The new coach has to work with all the players that were there before, but address the existing issues in a new way.

It made me realize that, no matter how dysfunctional my districts may have been when I arrived, I couldn't fire my way out of the problem. There were certain people here and there who needed to be replaced, but there were four thousand employees in Elizabeth, and two thousand in Passaic. There was no way that I could make a clean sweep, replace everyone, and miraculously change everything in the schools. Even if it were logistically and financially possible, it would be chaotic, demoralizing, and totally counterproductive.

Instead, I had to change the people from the inside out. In order to make significant improvements that would affect the students' experiences and outcomes, we needed to invest time and energy in professional development for everyone: teachers, administrators, and staff at every level. We had to grow our teachers' skills in pedagogy and mastery of the content. We worked with staff to grow their management and leadership skills, from principals and assistant principals to supervisors of the custodial teams, and everyone in between.

I'll talk more about the specifics of professional development in Chapter Five. For now, here's the point I want to leave you with: a big part of walking out my vision for excellence was to equip my employees to perform with excellence. Helping everyone level up, leveled up our culture.

You can't fire your way out of a culture problem. You must develop and transform the people you already have.

PUT YOUR VISION INTO ACTION

Your vision and mission will direct the programs you develop for your district. A low-performing district that expects very little from its students will not offer rigorous programs that help them succeed. You may have a few bright, motivated kids here and there who get special attention and wind up going to good colleges. Systematically, there is nothing in place that's designed to give everyone a realistic shot at Harvard or Yale. In a culture of low performance, the very concept would be considered ridiculous. But that lack of vision is precisely what holds the district back from creating those opportunities.

You begin by deciding what sort of school district you want to have. What outcomes do you want for your students? That will dictate the policies you put in place. Your vision, mission, and policies then inform the programs that you'll offer. This aspect of educational leadership is close to my heart because one of the jobs I loved best was as the director of curriculum and instruction in Elizabeth, before I moved up to assistant superintendent and then superintendent, a.k.a. "supe."

Later, when I became superintendent of schools in Passaic, we had no written programs of study, nothing that the board had approved. Every teacher was teaching what they wanted in their classroom. Schools were selecting their own books. Initially, I did what I could to move us toward becoming a college-going school district, but my options were limited.

That intention became part of our vision and mission, and creating cohesive programs of study was the first step. I got my assistant superintendent and my director of elementary and secondary instruction on board, and charged them with creating the plans we needed: programs of study, a textbook approval list, a curriculum list, and a five-year curriculum plan to revise and update our curriculum on a cycle. None of those things existed—my team had to create them from scratch.

Once we captured and documented everything we were doing that year, we started revising it so that we could evolve every year a bit closer to our vision of college and career readiness for every student. It took a year or two for all the policies we wanted to be approved by the board and put in place, so it was a gradual process.

One of the first academic moves we made was to require algebra for all eighth graders. Before that, they might not encounter it until ninth grade. Over time, that changed the requirements for seventh grade, and eventually we had more and more seventh graders taking algebra and eighth graders taking geometry. Those changed requirements had to be backed up with planning, budgets, and making sure the students were prepared in earlier grades for the material.

Our vision for getting all students into honors classes and Advanced Placement classes also required policy changes. Left to their own devices, most teachers, administrators, and guidance counselors would put up all kinds of hurdles that kept kids out of those rigorous advanced classes. I killed all those prerequisites, because they stood directly in the way of our vision and mission.

This was my Leader's Algorithm at work: we had an ultimate goal of preparing students for high achievement. High achievement requires academic rigor, so I had to put that theory into practice by offering rigorous courses and removing barriers for students to take them.

Put your vision into action through policies and programs that serve your students.

The performance of your students is the result of your district's culture. Your culture is the result of your vision and mission, and how faithfully you walk them out. A lack of vision or a limited vision for your district's future create low expectations for your students. A big vision for the future and a focus on excellence create high expectations and deliver high achievement.

What do you expect from your administrators, teachers, and students? We'll take a deeper look at the power of your expectations in Chapter Three.

CHAPTER 3

LEADING THROUGH EXPECTATIONS

"From everyone who has been given much, much will be demanded; and from the one who has been entrusted with much, much more will be asked."

—LUKE 12:48

All the way back in kindergarten, when that teacher predicted I would be held back, she wasn't pulling it out of nowhere. In reality, I had a lot stacked against me. I didn't know my colors in English, but there were also a lot of other things I didn't realize about my family. I didn't know that my mom wasn't yet fully literate in English. I had no idea that some of my relatives couldn't read and write in Spanish, either. Most importantly, I didn't know how lucky I was to have the parents—and extended family—that I got.

Throughout my life, I encountered authority figures with low expectations, from kindergarten, through high school, all the way up to attending Yale as a first-generation college student.

People predicted I would fail. Worse yet, they were patronizing when I succeeded. People made condescending, racist remarks (sometimes even thinking they were being funny and friendly). What they didn't count on—what I only later learned to appreciate—was that the strength of my family's expectations dwarfed everything else.

When my dad's passion for baseball inspired me to play on a real team, he contacted every league in the area, and nobody would take me. I don't believe the leagues made that decision capriciously. Extracurricular sports take a lot of time, money, and parental support. Both my parents worked full time in lower-wage jobs. They didn't have a lot of time or money to spare. A lot of kids in my position couldn't even attend practices consistently, much less play at a high level. But my father made it happen anyway.

My mother believed that I was smart and capable, and that I could learn anything in the world if I studied. She drilled me on my colors, and everything else I needed to know. My father believed that I was talented and motivated, and that I could be a champion if I practiced. He never stopped looking for a Little League that would take a chance on me, and he found a great one. All the low expectations around me couldn't get inside me, because of the faith and encouragement that my parents poured into me.

Many kids aren't so lucky. Most kids aren't going to take low expectations as a challenge and set out to prove everyone wrong. If their confidence and self-belief isn't being nurtured somehow, it will shrivel up and die. School may be the only place children get told that they are intelligent, they have a bright future, and they're capable of greatness. And if they have high expectations at home *and* at school, guess what? They can rise even higher.

I'll tell you another secret: it works on grown-ups just the same. Holding staff, teachers, and students to high expectations has no downside and all upside.

When you dream big, you inspire bold action.

BIG AND BOLD

Author Ken Blanchard wrote, "The key to successful leadership is influence, not authority." That's exactly the position a superintendent is in when it comes to making systemic changes to the school district. The bigger and bolder your aspirations, the more you require influence to turn your proposals into policies. The supe has a certain amount of authority over district employees, but you don't have a vote on the board. You must also deal with many different stakeholders and political interests—the unions, local politicians, parents, and community leaders.

As we discussed in Chapter One, one of the strongest reasons to make your personal Theory of Action public is so your stakeholders can see your ultimate goal and understand how your individual decisions and actions will lead the organization to it. Putting your expectations in black and white makes them that much more compelling and persuasive. It also seeds important conversations with your stakeholders. They don't need to figure you out or try to deduce your intentions—it's all right there on the table for discussion.

During my superintendency in Elizabeth, I attended the Broad Superintendent's Academy (now The Broad Center at Yale School of Management). My mentor, Tom Payzant, had served as the superintendent in Oklahoma City; Eugene, Oregon; San Diego; and at the time was the superintendent in Boston. At one point he asked me to guess which job had been most challenging in terms of getting things done.

Now, Boston had about sixty thousand students enrolled at the time, but San Diego had over a hundred thousand. I said that San Diego must have been the hardest place to make progress. He said, "No, not at all. Boston was the hardest."

I couldn't imagine why, since the scale was so much smaller. "Because the list of people I have to call is so much longer," he said. In San Diego he could use his influence with a small number of people to leverage the whole district toward change. In Boston, he needed to speak with and persuade so many more people that it was much harder to accomplish anything he wanted to do.

In your district, you may have to speak with a few key leaders on the board, or you may need to persuade everyone from the president of the PTO to a local pastor to the city council president. Whether your calling list is short or long, the key to influencing change is to present an uplifting and emotionally compelling set of expectations.

HEARTS AND MINDS

When you set out bold expectations for your district and your students, aim to win hearts before you try to persuade their minds. You may have all the rational reasons in the world why a change is for the best, but it takes emotional reasons to move people to change. Buy-in happens emotionally before it can happen intellectually, so your big dreams need to be big enough to bring everyone else along with you. Personally, I gravitate toward facts and research, and you need those cognitive, rational triggers on your side. But when you need to take bold action, finding the right emotional trigger can get people over the hump.

When I arrived in Passaic, I wanted to move the district to a K–8 configuration instead of having a freestanding middle school, because research showed that it was beneficial for the students' development and academic confidence. I thought it would give us a strong inflection point to raise standards for all the students.

Well, the board was accustomed to the elementary-middle-high school arrangement. The idea of putting middle schoolers with elementary—or even to move the other way and create 6–12 schools by placing middle schoolers with high school—was such a huge change that the research didn't convince them. They were uncomfortable with the idea, which is an emotional response.

So instead, I did a different kind of research. I made a list of all the best schools in the country (according to *US News & World Report* and the *Washington Post*) that had eliminated middle schools and moved to a 6–12 or K–8 format. Suddenly, the board started thinking differently. They saw that these schools were great and they wanted to be great, too. They wanted to see our district on that list, so they agreed to take a chance on change.

The bolder your dream, the more emotionally compelling it must be.

EXPECTING EXCELLENCE

In Chapter Two, we discussed how a focus on academic excellence and rigor can raise expectations for students overall, while low expectations are demoralizing. Wherever you set your expectations, they will become a self-fulfilling prophecy.

In order to turn around the performance of the Elizabeth and Passaic districts, we had to build in high expectations at every level. Our ultimate goal was to graduate college- and career-ready students who could compete for high paying jobs. Our concrete objective was to improve teaching and learning by moving to a managed or Aligned Instructional System. That meant leveraging **3 Ps: Policies**, **Programs**, and **Personnel**.

In terms of **personnel**, we selected and developed administrators to be leaders who would inspire excellence in teaching, learning, and discipline. We also selected and developed teachers who would provide challenging academic tasks for the students.

We created board **policies** on attendance, promotion, retention, grading, and graduation that articulated clear and rigorous standards. We pushed for more Gifted and Talented (G&T) programs (including standalone G&T schools) and created new programs of study. At the high school level, we added Advanced Placement and dual-enrollment college classes.

When you raise expectations, you must also provide supportive **programs** to equip your students so they can meet those expectations. In order to help our students advance, we added before- and after-school tutoring, Saturday school, and summer programming to bridge the gaps.

Eventually, this synergy of people, policies, and programs generated momentum that propelled the whole district forward. In his book *Good to Great*, Jim Collins describes this process as the Flywheel Effect: the cumulative impact of many actions, repeated over time, gathers force until it reaches a tipping point. Once the momentum takes over, the weight of the wheel continues turning faster and faster while you only expend the same amount of effort. That's what happened with our district changes—the initial push of getting buy-in was compounded by every action that helped to raise expectations and support the staff and students. Then the new expectations of excellence became self-perpetuating, as students began to think of themselves as high achievers and live out that belief every day.

Your expectations guide your actions. Your actions perpetuate your expectations.

INSTRUCTIONAL CORE

During the 2008–2009 school year, I joined the Panasonic Foundation in launching the New Jersey Network of Superintendents. Our goal was to advance educational equity by improving instruction. Through this work, I was introduced to the concept of the instructional core, which created a real breakthrough in my ideas on how to set high academic standards and help students meet them.

The instructional core is described in *Instructional Rounds in Education*.[6] It consists of three elements, which are all connected and which all influence each other:

- The skill and knowledge of the teacher,
- Student engagement, and
- Challenging content.

These three elements converge around a specific learning task. In other words, the instructional core is the teaching-and-learning process that happens in the classroom. There are several key principles to improving the instructional core. Two of those principles had a particular impact on my thinking and my approach to educational leadership.

First, if you work on one element of the instructional core, you must also work on the other two elements. They can't be addressed in isolation. For example, if you want the student to engage with more rigorous content, you must ensure that the teacher fully understands the content and is prepared with the right skills to present it. The student must be motivated to engage with their own learning, and that engagement comes from their relationship with the teacher, the content, and the task.

The second major principle is that task predicts performance. Let me repeat that, because it's the most important: **task predicts**

---

6 Elizabeth A. City, Richard F. Elmore, Sarah E. Fiarman, and Lee Teitel. *Instructional Rounds in Education: A Network Approach to Improving Teaching and Learning*, Cambridge, MA: Harvard Education Press, 2009.

performance. This is true for the students, the teachers, the staff as a whole, and for you! In much the same way that I repeated vision, mission, and guiding principles to my staff and stakeholders, I constantly repeated this phrase in my districts. I encourage you to make it your mantra.

The students' daily tasks will predict their performance on tests and in their future coursework. It doesn't matter what the lesson plan says, or what the teacher directed the students to do. What matters is the *actual* task the student is doing. To improve instruction, you must give the students engaging, cognitively challenging tasks to work on—which requires rigorous content and skilled teachers. You see? It's a cycle, and everything converges on the task. We'll talk more about improving the instructional core in Chapter Five, "Leading with Skills."

Just as preparation predicts execution for your personal Theory of Action, task predicts performance for your students.

SETTING POLICIES

While you implement your personal Theory of Action in your district, I urge you to advocate for your board to enact an organizational TOA as an official policy. It may take some persuasion, but setting an organizational TOA at the board policy level will become the backbone of your long-term strategic plan for the district. Superintendents change. Board members change. Resolutions can be conceived and passed in one night, and revoked just as quickly. If you want your organizational

TOA to make substantive changes in the district, it needs to become policy.

Policies require more reflection and discussion, multiple board meetings to discuss and create alignment, and more votes in order to pass—which means more commitment from the school board. It's like the difference between an executive order from the White House, which can change with the stroke of a pen, and a piece of legislation that has to be negotiated and passed by both houses of Congress. Once your organizational TOA becomes policy, you, your staff, and the board can refer to it frequently, and it will guide all your work.

In addition to the organizational Theory of Action, I also found certain practical policy changes to be crucial for improving student learning: the code of student conduct (including attendance), raising high school graduation requirements, and updating standards for promotion, retention, grading, and reporting.

Neither of my districts had updated their governance manuals in decades, so it was quite a revelation when I started going through all the existing policies and creating uniformity among the schools. Because everything was so far out of date, the administrators had been on their own to make up and apply their own standards in each school. The principals each had their own rules and systems of discipline, so we created a consistent framework of progressive discipline for specified infractions.

The real levers for teaching and learning came in updating the high school graduation requirements. On my recommendation, the board passed a requirement for more credit hours than the state minimum. That meant the students were taking more English, more math, and more science. We also passed policies that required coursework at the college prep or higher level. Then we eliminated the low-level tracked classes, because they wouldn't meet graduation requirements. The students who had been scraping by at the state minimums were mainstreamed into classes with the rest of the student body. This was an important change to improve equity and expand opportunities for all students.

Finally, we set a requirement that every student must take a college entrance exam, such as the SAT or an equivalent. Then those requirements helped us build our programs and curriculum, because we had to make sure that students were offered the necessary prerequisites and preparatory instruction so that they could succeed in the higher-level coursework. Together, all these changes moved us toward our objective of Managed Instruction and our ultimate goal of making our students competitive in the marketplace.

The strongest demonstration of your board's commitment to excellence is to adopt an organizational TOA as official policy.

INNOVATIVE CHOICES

When designing a challenging program—particularly one focused on college and career readiness—it's essential that you give students and parents options for courses of study that are engaging and relevant to the students' gifts and interests. Some districts use an organizational TOA that emphasizes complete school choice and a strong network of charter schools. If you look at my organizational TOAs for Elizabeth and Passaic, you'll see that I felt strongly about Managed Instruction and cohesive instructional systems, but at the same time I lean toward Performance Empowerment.[7]

Performance Empowerment refers to the fact that it was necessary at the outset to build a strong central office and set uniform standards to support and develop administrators and teachers. The goal of that development was to grow the administrators' skills and leadership, and then release them to make more and more independent decisions about programs and personnel. If a group is underperforming, you aren't doing them any favors by delegating a lot of authority to them. First, you need to grow their capacity and ability. Then, as they build a track record of success, you can give them more autonomy.

To offer our students relevant and interesting choices, we got creative. In Elizabeth, we developed several themed magnet schools for grades K–8 that enrolled students by lottery, as well as two grade 2–8 Gifted and Talented schools that selected students based on an application. Our themed schools included a STEAM academy, an International Baccalaureate academy, and a leadership academy that was based on the principles of *The 7 Habits of Highly Effective People*. Our largest high school was split into six interest-based academies, some for the arts and finance, some for technical careers, and two that required

---

[7] Donald R. McAdams. *What School Boards Can Do: Reform Governance for Urban Schools*, New York, NY: Teachers College Press, 2006.

students to take a full course load of advanced or AP classes for all four years.

Passaic, being a smaller district, had only one grade 2–8 Gifted and Talented school. The former middle school was converted into two themed academies for grades 6–12, and our comprehensive high school became a career and technical academy with ten different themed programs.

All these programs focused on improving the instructional core. The choice of interest and career content increased parent involvement and student engagement. It allowed students to work on tasks and projects that were directly tied to their individual dreams and aspirations. Since task predicts performance, we could predict that they would perform better in their future careers. The specialized programs also led teachers to develop in particular areas of strength so their knowledge and skills could grow, too.

Choice increases engagement, expands content, develops teachers' skills, and improves the instructional core.

TIME IS PRECIOUS

Both my districts needed large-scale changes, but I didn't want to walk in and blow everything up—when that happens, the people on the ground don't wind up owning the changes. I needed to get deep into the organization and understand the people, their needs, and the dynamics. My leadership style is to approach change in a slow and deliberate manner so that the policies and programs we plant can develop deep roots and last long after my tenure as supe is over. That's why I only had two demands when I negotiated my employment contracts with the board. The most important element was time. For most people, salary and perks matter, but to me, nothing outweighed the value of time to implement change. I wanted to be guaranteed enough time to see my initiatives bear fruit. (I'll tell you the second demand later.)

I spent eight and a half years in Elizabeth, and seven and a half in Passaic, systematically introducing changes throughout that time. As deliberate as those plans were, the changes felt very fast to many stakeholders because they were so far-reaching and changed the status quo. Still, it's a snail's pace compared to some famous (or infamous) turnaround artists you may see in the news, who made tumultuous changes and got fired quickly. I followed—and recommend—the model of my mentor, Tom Payzant, who spent eleven years transforming the Boston school district. As he showed me, taking the time to invest in relationships and thoughtful, step-by-step changes can make a huge difference for winning long-term buy-in and making improvements stick.

The bolder your dream, the more time you need to make it come true.

RISING TO THE CHALLENGE

Students can do what you ask them to do. You just have to believe in them and in your goals—and that belief manifests in the way you put structures and supports into place. When your academics are strong, and particularly when your sports teams are strong and your marching band is strong, you provide multiple areas where students can succeed. This atmosphere of success helps to stabilize the school, because kids enjoy the comradery of participating and winning. Sometimes the most troubled students can be refocused through extracurricular activities, and by investing in those activities they get motivated to keep their grades up.

You also see students policing themselves. We offer adult leaders in the schools, but the students will also find student leaders to follow. If those leaders are focused on their academic work and extracurricular activities, and their success is acknowledged, that creates a strong influence on their peers. Perhaps there's official recognition with blue ribbons on Awards Day. Perhaps word gets around about their college plans. Perhaps your athletes win championships and All-State recognition. The presence of successful student leaders helps the other students become inspired and encourage each other to rise to the challenge.

That doesn't mean every student is thrilled with your requirements all the time. You're asking students to work hard, and working hard is hard work. You can expect to hear some complaints and criticism. The way you handle that criticism can give your students positive expectations for you.

Let me give you an example: in Elizabeth, we had two high schools that wound up with high rankings in the annual school surveys by the *Washington Post, Newsweek,* and *US News & World Report*—Elizabeth High School and Hamilton Prep. At both schools, we set the requirement that all students had to take a full course load as long as they were enrolled, even if they had already earned enough credits to graduate. We had nine or ten class periods in the day, and the students had to take a full schedule all the way to graduation.

One day I was walking past the athletic fields with some colleagues, and a student sitting on the ground with her friends recognized me by name. I asked how I could help her, and she clearly wasn't happy.

She asked, "Why are you making me take a full load my senior year? I only need a few more credits."

I replied, "That's an excellent question. I made that requirement because I want you prepared for the world outside high school. I hope that you'll go on to college and complete college. When you leave here and go to college, and then get a job, you'll be competing against people with academic and financial advantages that you and I didn't have. I want you to get as much instruction—rigorous instruction—as you possibly can before you leave high school, because that's what your peers in the suburbs are getting.

"I know you're unhappy with me now, but in a few years when you graduate college and get a great job because I made you study harder and take more classes, I hope you'll see how it helped you."

She didn't come back at me, so I hope that my reasons made sense to her. Often, people will accept a leader's decisions as long as they know there's a good reason for them (even if they don't like them). Young people in particular resent requirements that appear arbitrary or capricious. I was glad she asked, because to me it was an easy question. Our ultimate goal was very clear in my personal TOA, and every decision I made about academic requirements was done to pursue that goal: *for our students to graduate prepared to pursue a college education; to think, learn, achieve, and care; and to receive high pay in the 21st century marketplace.*

My biggest dream in my sixteen years as a superintendent was to make the Gifted and Talented curriculum the default curriculum for all students in kindergarten through eighth grade, and to make Advanced Placement the default curriculum at the high school level. I got closer and closer to fulfilling it, but we never quite got all the way there. We were able to move from having a few hundred AP exams to more than two thousand per year. That led to more and more students taking AP classes, and more of them scoring threes, fours, and fives on their AP exams.

I was disappointed that we weren't able to provide that opportunity to every student in our district, but by aiming for the top of the chart we were able to make substantive changes and radically expand access for thousands of students. They say that if you shoot for the moon and miss, you still land among the stars. Even if you don't fully achieve your dream, you can change expectations—and change lives—on a massive scale.

> In Appendix D you can see real-world data on how our high aims resulted in great leaps in student achievement.

Students can do whatever you ask them to do—so think deeply about what you're asking.

EXPECTATIONS FOR THE LEADER

When you set high expectations for your team and your students, they will also have high expectations of you. Indeed, the public nature of your Leader's Algorithm encourages them to do so. My formative lessons in leadership came from my parents—the way Dad coached me, the way Mom encouraged me, and the way they both uplifted me with their expectations. They are reserved people, quiet in their talk, so I learned more from their actions than their words. That quiet nature set my very first expectation for leadership:

Listen and learn with your eyes and heart, more than with your ears.

Based on my parents' example, and confirmed by experiences throughout my career, I believe leadership rests on five main principles: commitment, high standards, faith, loyalty, and humility.

COMMITMENT

My dad was dedicated to practicing with me no matter how tired he may have been or how little spare time he had. He was also rabidly committed to getting me onto a Little League team. As a matter of fact, he faked our residency in the next town over so I could join their team. (It was the 1970s. I think the statute of limitations has probably run out on Little League fraud by now.)

Dad's work schedule made it difficult for him to attend my games, so Mom was the one who drove me and attended 99 percent of them. Together, their total commitment to developing my talent and giving me opportunities inspired me to trust and follow them, and carried me through the hard work of practice and playing. Baseball wasn't just a game. It was an opportunity to connect with my father's passion, so it became my passion too.

HIGH STANDARDS

When that young lady at Elizabeth called me out about requiring a full course load, I understood how she felt. There can be a love-hate relationship with a leader who holds you to a high standard. My father was rigorous and uncompromising in pushing me to develop my skills. Getting critiqued by your dad isn't fun, and he could be hard on me. In the long run, the discomfort of those challenges paid off, and I respect and appreciate the high standards Dad set for me.

In the same way that my mother refused to let me fail kindergarten, she refused to let me quit college. My freshman year at Yale was tough on many levels, and at one point I called home to tell Mom I wanted to "take a break" (what I really wanted to do was drop out).

Her response was quick and to the point: "No. You are staying in school. Your dad and I worked too hard so you could go to college, for you to quit now. No! You will stay, finish, and graduate in four years. I believe in you. I have faith in you!"

FAITH

Mom was right. Her standards seemed impossibly high to me at the time, but her unwavering faith made them come true. Her faith in me enabled me to keep going. Eventually, it created faith in myself.

No matter how tired I might be from long practices or irritated by Dad's critique, I understood where he was coming from. My father believed I was capable of playing in the major leagues, and he made me believe it too. His drive to help me advance was tireless. His encouragement was constant. His willingness to find and pursue opportunities for me demonstrated the depth of his faith in me and my abilities. Even when I doubted myself, he had enough faith for both of us.

As a leader, your faith in your team and your students is a great gift that empowers them to succeed.

Faith is a major theme in my leadership story:

- My family's faith in me, and mine in them;
- Faith in my team, staff, and students; and
- Faith in God and his divine guidance in my life.

How has faith (your own and others') guided and supported you throughout your life? How can you demonstrate faith in your team and your students?

LOYALTY

My dad appreciated the teams that accepted me and invested in me, and his commitment to me extended in a commitment to those teams. By the time I was in middle school, I was playing on two different teams. The St. Joseph's team was the first to accept me, so I'd been playing with them for a few years. When my cousin Carlos and I got a reputation as good players, other teams were interested in taking us on. We wound up playing for a second team closer to home in Elizabeth, but a conflict arose when we made All-Star for both teams and were headed to the same tournament.

We had to make a choice. It felt great to be in demand! And the Elizabeth team practiced "right around the corner," so choosing their All-Star team would have been the path of least resistance. Nevertheless, St. Joseph's had taken a chance on us when nobody else would, so we stuck with them. It was pretty strange to play against the kids from Elizabeth—our neighbors and teammates—but it was the right thing to do. My mom and dad never talked about loyalty directly, but they modeled it in consistent choices that valued relationships over convenience or ego.

HUMILITY

My parents have a great deal of dignity, but they are never arrogant or boastful. They were hard workers in their professions. They are caring parents. They did what they could with the educational level they had. If they ever bragged, they bragged about their children (and now their grandchildren and great grandchildren). I was able to visit my dad's workplace many times through the years, and I always heard the same two things from his coworkers: The first was, "You have a great dad!" The second was, "He talks about you all the time."

When I was younger, he talked about school and baseball, and later college. Later, he talked about how I became a teacher and eventually a superintendent. All through the different phases of life, he talked about how well I was doing, but he never bragged about himself in any way.

In fact, he did the opposite: he quietly worked behind the scenes to help others, in ways that nobody ever saw or acknowledged. After a rainy night, if I had a Little League game the next day, he would get up early before work to prepare the field. We played on sandlots, and most of the rainwater would drain until it hit a low point, where you'd get a puddle. If that puddle stood on the field too close to game time, you wouldn't be able to move the water around and aerate the field. You'd just get a soupy mess and the field would be unplayable.

My dad grew up on a farm and understood the way sand and soil perc after a rain. It was intuitive for him that the field needed to be raked early in the day so the water could drain properly and dry the field in time for the game. After a late night at the restaurant, he'd get up early to drive me to school, and then go straight over to the ball field to rake it. After a day of sun, it would be dry by five or six in the evening. My mom thought he was crazy to be up doing manual labor at that hour, after a long night working. He'd just say he wanted me to get my game in.

Nobody else knew. I didn't even understand what he was doing until much later when Coach Korn told me. The fields would just magically be dry whenever we needed them, and thirty kids—most of whom my dad didn't even know—would get their game in.

Humility—listening more than you talk, serving without craving credit for it, bragging on other people's accomplishments instead of your own—is a crucial quality for healthy, effective leadership, and it's demonstrated far too rarely in the public or private sector. So many in our society think of "leadership potential" as an innate gift of charisma or heroism, but that couldn't be further from the truth. It takes daily practice, trying and failing and learning from failures before you succeed. Good leaders have to work at it, and they have to stay humble.

Think back to your own experiences of good and bad leaders. What principles can you take away from those mentors and models (or cautionary tales)? What does excellent leadership look like to you?

EXCELLENCE FOR EVERYONE

Traditional thinking in underperforming systems views high achievers as rare and exceptional. There's a kernel of truth there, since it is rare for people to buck the pressure of low expectations and achieve great things in spite of them. These outliers are polished up and presented as the stars of a broken system.

I want to challenge that whole worldview. I never saw my students as divided into higher-performing and lower-performing groups. I saw them inside the whole macro system of education.

I didn't compare them against each other, but I compared their opportunities and preparation against the opportunities available to students in affluent communities. I thought about our students when they left home and needed to compete in the global marketplace.

That's why I had a higher aspiration for my students. We couldn't create a school district that would serve and highlight a few star pupils while we let down the rest. We needed to design a system that would uplift everyone, because every single one of those students deserves the best we could possibly offer. When we redesigned those systems to expect and support excellence from every student, we created new trajectories of success in their lives and for their families.

Low expectations increase disparities. High expectations elevate everyone.

In case you were wondering, the second element I insisted on when negotiating my employment contracts was that I could choose my own administrative team—the people I needed to work through to accomplish anything else. In order to carry out your personal TOA and fulfill your expectations for excellence, you need the right team to help you put it all into practice. That's the focus of our next chapter, "Leading through Teamwork."

CHAPTER 4

LEADING THROUGH TEAMWORK

> *"I can do things you cannot, you can do things I cannot; together we can do great things."*
>
> —MOTHER TERESA

My senior year in high school, my baseball team lost the state championship over a hat.

I was pitching and forced the batter to hit a ground ball. I reached for it, but then I pulled back because it was headed straight to the second baseman. Since he was actually standing near the base, catching that grounder could have given us an easy double play. Game over, we'd win and take home the trophy for the second year in a row.

Just at that moment, the second baseman started to lose his cap. He grabbed for the hat and missed the ball. Instead of a winning play, we wound up with the bases loaded.

A few pitches later, I walked a batter, advancing the winning run for the other team. I ended up as the losing pitcher. But it wasn't my fault—it was the second baseman grabbing his stupid cap!

Or was it?

Let's rewind that game. Earlier on, we were leading by a big margin—five to nothing. We were hitting, and I was a runner at first base. The first base coach thought it was going to rain soon, so he wanted to speed up the game to make it official before it got rained out. He told me, "We need to create some outs here." He thought our lead was safe, so we didn't need to continue scoring runs, steal bases, or play offense aggressively. He didn't anticipate that we'd fall apart in the bottom of the seventh inning.

Our starting pitcher was a superstar who was throwing over ninety miles an hour (and wound up getting drafted to the Kansas City Royals). By the seventh inning, he was out of gas. I was the relief pitcher, the closer, but instead of bringing me in, Coach brought in our third baseman. He had a wicked fastball too (and was later drafted by the Atlanta Braves), but he didn't have the same level of control and accuracy. The other team scored a bunch of runs and got runners on base.

By the time Coach finally brought me in to pitch, we'd gone from five-nothing, to five to four with runners on first and second bases. My first batter was the ground ball that should have ended the game. My second and third walked, and we lost the championship—the game we'd been winning with a huge lead—six to five. I cried from the pitcher's mound to the bus, as I felt I let down my teammates. We traveled from Princeton to Elizabeth in silence, staring out the bus windows as we rode on Route 1. And just to add insult to injury, it didn't rain.

Throughout that game, there were decisions and reversals of circumstance that could have thrown the outcome one way or another. So, who lost the game for us? The first-base coach, who got cocky about our lead and wanted to speed up the game instead of scoring as many runs as possible? The head coach who changed strategy and put in the third baseman before his established closer? Was it the pitcher who gave away all those runs, or the second baseman who got distracted by his hat? Or was it me, who failed to pitch a strike when it mattered the most?

None of the above. All of the above. We were a team. When we won games, we won as a team. When we lost, we lost as a team. We were all disappointed, but we didn't turn on each other. We had strong, loyal relationships on and off the field, and we hung together in victory and defeat. That loyalty and cohesion were cultivated by our coach Ray Korn, and made us stronger together than any of us could be on our own. Coach Korn knew that teamwork was more important in the long run than any one game, or even any one year's championship. History proved him right, because he earned a lifetime record for his high school coaching career, and a spot in the American Baseball Coaches Association Hall of Fame.

He understood that leadership is delivering results with and through other people, and that it is vital to nurture your people.

CREATING WINNING TEAMS

The coach's role is different for teams that play at different levels.

An excellent coach for little kids teaches them the game. As players mature, the coach needs to develop their talent and put them in the role that best leverages their abilities to help the team win. When you reach an elite or professional level, the head coach must manage the relationships between players and keep them working together as a seamless unit (which isn't easy when you're dealing with millionaire celebrities and their egos). A club full of incredible talent with bad chemistry or interpersonal friction won't win, because they don't play as a team—they are just a bunch of prima donnas on the field.

The same is true in education. Teachers lead students in their tasks. Administrators develop and manage individuals on the teams within their schools. The superintendent manages teams of teams, and the relationship dynamics of the system as a whole. You must select key people who can understand and deliver on your personal Theory of Action, both in improving instruction and in managing the teams under them.

THE RIGHT PEOPLE IN THE RIGHT PLACE

Your Leader's Algorithm defines how you will deliver on your vision and mission. Selecting your management team is one of the first things on your list of priorities, and your leadership criteria may need revision along the way just like all the other components of your personal TOA. If you aren't reaching the results you projected, sometimes your personal TOA is correct but you have the wrong people in the wrong places to carry it out. You must be thoughtful and intentional about how you design your organization, how you select the people to help you run it, how you develop people, and how you form teams.

One of the most important questions to ask yourself about a candidate is, "Can they lead, and will people follow?"

We all have different personality types, strengths, and weaknesses. Leaders come in different forms, so you need to build a team that complements you and each other. Make sure you seek out people who are smarter and better than you—especially in your areas of weakness—so you can cover all the bases.

I referred to my core management team as my cabinet. My priorities for selecting cabinet members are that they focus on the vision and mission, lead with a commitment to improve classroom instruction, exhibit excellent teamwork, merit trust, and share my high expectations for student achievement. I believe those qualities would be valuable in any organization, but you may need to emphasize a different set of priorities based on the needs of your district and your personal blind spots or challenges.

To serve your district well, you need to function as an orchestra conductor, not a one-man band. When you select and develop a strong, cohesive team of leaders who can develop and manage teams of their own, you can manage their timing and balance, harmonize their efforts, and harness their creativity to produce beautiful results. You won't need to run around huffing and puffing, trying to toot all the horns yourself.

To achieve your ultimate goal, you need to select the right people, in the right places, with the right strengths, for the right reasons.

BALANCING TEAMS

In Chapter Two I mentioned that you can't fire your way out of a culture problem. When you're working in a school district—or any large organization—you have to be realistic about the talents of the team members you inherit, and think strategically about where to place them. A mentor of mine from the Elizabeth district, Rafael Fajardo, used to say, "You go to war with the army you have!" Your goal is to make the best teams and subteams that you can, with the resources that you have available.

In my superintendencies, I would work with my cabinet to design the strongest administrative teams we could find for each school. Whenever a vacancy would arise, we'd look at our roster of principals, vice or assistant principals, teacher coaches, instructional supervisors, and leaders at all levels to try to find people with the experience, temperament, and abilities that were needed most in the context of a particular school.

Naturally, every administrator wasn't blessed with top talent and skill in every possible area. We had a broad spectrum of abilities in management, instruction, and leadership. There were some excellent, some poor, and most were in the middle. So the cabinet and I would try to combine people in different roles to create the strongest overall team for each school. The largest schools with many layers of administration were actually the easiest, because with multiple assistant principals there were more opportunities for team members to support each other and balance each other out. The small schools were the hardest because often the principal wouldn't have an administrative team and would be working on their own.

TEACHING AND LEADING

Working inside the constraints of public-school staffing, moving people around isn't enough. You also need to develop the leaders you have so they can acquire the skillsets they need. In Elizabeth, I managed 120 administrators, and in Passaic it was just under a hundred. About 90 percent of them were instructional administrators, and the rest dealt with back-office functions. In selecting those instructional administrators, I always focused on two things: teaching and leading.

A principal may not teach in the classroom, but they need to know what good teaching looks like. They need to understand rigorous instruction. They need to be able to teach their team members and help them improve in pedagogy and understanding content—to help their teachers become better teachers.

As leaders, it's essential that principals can deliver results. Will people follow them? Beyond that, can they become self-replicating leaders—will they identify and develop future leaders among their own staff?

Interestingly, when looking for operational administrators and team members, the questions don't change that much. They still need to be able to teach, because they must assess the skills of their staff, train their staff on best practices, and help them level up any skill gaps. Whether they work with the custodial staff, IT, or finance, administrators still need to teach and lead their people so that they can all help bring us closer to our ultimate goal.

I had one principal who is a great manager, in terms of keeping everything running smoothly. He's a great leader when it comes to inspiring people to deliver results and helping to identify, support, and promote talent on his team. Unfortunately, he's not a very good teacher.

On the plus side, he is smart and humble enough to know that he needs to lean on his instructional people to fill that gap in his own abilities. So to balance his team, I made sure to give him vice principals (VPs) who were strong on instruction. If a vacancy showed up where I moved a vice principal on, I made sure to assign him someone who could step in and keep that gap covered.

With other principals who were very strong on instruction, I might assign them a vice principal who was weaker in that area. In any skillset, we looked for ways to match principals and VPs with complementary strengths and weaknesses. That matchup has two benefits: it keeps the teams balanced and creates an opportunity for that weaker VP to learn and develop from the principal's mentorship. These mentoring principals become a pipeline for new leaders, as the vice principals they develop get promoted to principal or get moved to help a weaker principal in turn.

Creating balanced teams doesn't just advance your vision and mission—it also creates a self-replicating chain of new and growing leaders.

CULTIVATING RELATIONSHIPS

As part of my Plan of Entry to each school district, I spent ninety days on a listening and learning tour. Naturally, that allowed me to meet community members and do a bit of political groundwork. I learned about governance, organizational capacity, public relations, operations, and finance, and all the other aspects of making the district run. Most importantly, that time was vital for discovering the strengths, weaknesses, needs, and dynamics of my team, as well as beginning to form relationships with them.

You need to invest time with your cabinet, your directors, your supervisors, and all the leaders in your organization—one-on-one as well as in groups. Ask questions about the status of the district: What's going well? What's going poorly? What are the current vision and mission, and do they feel the system is on track to achieve them?

The big question I always ask is how my team members think we should improve teaching and learning. Then I sit back to see if anyone has ideas, or has a clear concept of how to discuss it. Even then, you need to see how they execute those theories and what kind of results they are delivering. Some people can talk a good game but can't put it into action. Others may not be able to articulate the elements of their practice and why it works, but may still be able to create excellent results.

It's also important to ask heart-led questions and get to know your team on a human level. Ask how their families are doing. Ask about their interests outside of work. As you listen, learn, and invest in relationships, make sure you're building those relationships in 360 degrees. You need to get to know your colleagues, your subordinates, your board, your students' parents, your union leaders, and your community leaders. You never know who talks to whom, so you need to cultivate positive connections everywhere you can. Every stakeholder in your system—whether they work for you or not—can be part of your team at some level.

TRUST IS PRICELESS

The importance of trust between a leader and their team was impressed on me when I was an assistant superintendent. My superintendent at the time had a strong personality and a tendency to yell when he wasn't happy about something. He called me into his office and started shouting at me. Honestly, I'm not entirely clear on what he was angry about. I think he was under the impression I had been talking to the school board behind his back, but I can't recall if he ever really told me the problem. He just kept saying, "I don't trust you! I don't trust you!"

I asked him, "Are you done?" Then I told him, "Trust is a two-way street. You don't trust me? Well, I don't trust you either."

It wasn't a model relationship, and that mutual lack of trust was at the heart of it. He was a highly political superintendent, so to him all relationships were transactional. He didn't place a high value on truth, authenticity, or even ability. Instead, trust for him meant relying on his subordinates to do as they were told, tow the party line, and back him up, right or wrong.

Over my sixteen years as a superintendent, I placed a very different emphasis on that two-way street of trust. While I was mindful of political necessities, I didn't primarily seek out team members who were good political operatives. Instead, I looked for passionate educators and leaders with integrity. Being able to trust my team meant trusting their judgment, motivations, values, and skills. I would tell new administrator hires or promotions up front that trust was a two-way street—I had to earn theirs, and they had to earn mine.

I wasn't always a warm-fuzzy boss, and there were occasions when I made someone cry. But it was always critical for me to be credible to my team, from my classroom teachers all the way to the school board. They could disagree with me, dislike me, have whatever feelings they might, but I was always honest with them. They might have a totally different perspective on the situation we were in or direction we should take, but they could have total confidence that I was speaking authentically and acting on our vision and mission. If anyone asked a question, they'd get a straight answer. Everything I said and did was founded on the best interests of the students, the staff, and the community.

If you don't build credibility at every step, then all your decisions—every word that comes out of your mouth—become suspect. In order to lead boldly and with excellence, people must believe in you and follow you. Transactional loyalty doesn't last.

There is no substitute for trust.

PROTECT YOUR TEAM

Remember, your team are your eyes and ears, your hands and feet—you depend on them to execute all the actions that will bring your ultimate goal into reality. As much as you rely on them, you must also protect them. When there is blowback on your vision and mission, political opposition, conflict with your stakeholders, or personal criticism, the leader must take those hits to spare the team.

One of my former assistant supes, Jeff Truppo, gave me a great compliment. After I retired and we reminisced about working together, he said, "Pablo, you went through a lot of things as superintendent that I had no idea about at the time." He was right. I had some strong opposition and some pretty dark periods as a result of absorbing all that flak. (I'll talk more about that in Chapter Seven). Jeff went on, "As many difficulties as you had, you were never difficult with me. Whatever I asked, you gave freely, and I never got the agita you were dealing with. You didn't pass it on to us."

It's one of the nicest things he could have said, because to my mind, that's exactly what a leader should do. Give your team the support and help they need to fulfill all the goals you're asking of them. Don't give them your worries and stress.

Keep your team focused on your ultimate goal by taking the hits for them. If you get grief, don't pass it on.

WIN AS A TEAM

Your personal Theory of Action is your plan to move your organization from its current state to your desired state. The route to get there isn't always clear. You can't move the organization where it needs to go, but your team can. When there are gaps in your plan, it depends on other people to fill them in. By developing healthy, complementary teams and cultivating mutual trust, you can create a wellspring of good ideas and capable leaders.

When your team knows that you have their backs, they will also have yours and each others'. With each person's talent leveraged in the right place, you can work as a cohesive unit. The path isn't always easy and there may be setbacks along the way, but if you face those losses as a team without pointing fingers, your relationships can grow stronger. Then you can win as a team, and keep on winning.

A championship team needs top-level skills, from the leader on down. To lead effectively, you must develop your own skills as a leader, and then create systematic opportunities for your team to develop, too. That's what we'll cover in Chapter Five.

CHAPTER 5

LEADING WITH SKILLS

"All I have learned, I learned from books."
—ABRAHAM LINCOLN

In my very first teaching job (which happened to be at Elizabeth High School) I also served as the freshman baseball coach. During the summers, I coached the Elizabeth American Legion team as well. Making the switch from player to coach required a completely different mindset. These positions totally changed my relationship to the game and allowed me to see leadership from both sides. I learned that a leader must constantly develop their skills, while also helping their team learn and grow.

Since Little League, I had focused on pitching. Even my first coaching opportunity was specialized, as a volunteer pitching coach. When it came time to coach the whole team, particularly as a head coach, I found that I needed to relearn a lot of general skills, as well as planning, strategy, and relationship management.

Head coaching requires you to break the whole game down into units and teach the players to develop their skills in every position. I had to go to clinics, read books, and watch videos on hitting, signaling, fielding, and all the defensive plays so I could teach them. I had to make decisions about lineups and when different players should go in and out to use their individual talents to the best advantage. I had to set up effective practices that helped my players progress in a systematic way.

I also had to learn the psychological aspects of developing relationships, motivating players, balancing personalities, and using the right combination of "carrot and stick" for each individual. I had to foster team cohesion and unity to build a great team that was more than the sum of its parts. Those abilities aren't just personality traits that you're born with (or not). They are interpersonal skills that a leader needs to develop and practice.

Just because I had played baseball my whole life didn't mean I knew how to coach it. Leadership is a process that you learn and refine over time. You must experience wins and losses, experiment with strategies and tactics, and develop insight into how best to nurture and deploy your team's talent. You don't start out being great at it. Sometimes you succeed and sometimes you fail, and you learn the most from your failures.

Great leadership is a growth process for you and your team.

To develop strong leadership skills, you need to create a personal definition of leadership, understand responsibility and authority, prepare yourself for excellence, and create a detailed plan. To develop your team's skills, you must create systematic, intentional learning opportunities, and lead your team by learning alongside them.

YOUR LEADERSHIP SKILLS

The role of a leader and the role of a manager or administrator often get confused. They are completely different concepts. Administrators have a daily to-do list of tasks to accomplish, while also solving everyday problems that arise for the teachers, parents, and students they deal with. They provide direction, resources, support, and accountability to make sure the work gets done.

Leaders make big-picture decisions about what work should be done and why. They identify the skills and talents needed to take the organization to its ultimate goal, and make plans to develop those skills in their team. They lead different groups in different ways, based on each group's needs and relationships.

But what is leadership, exactly? That's a question you have to answer for yourself.

DEFINING LEADERSHIP

One of the most valuable exercises in my leadership training at The Broad Academy was to write a personal definition of leadership. This was a challenge for me, because even though I had some excellent leaders in my life, I had never had a mentor within my field to help me understand the role. My mentors were books. Throughout my career, I read anything I could get my hands on about the nature and practice of leadership, particularly John Maxwell and Jim Collins, as well as biographies and memoirs of leaders in business, politics, and social reform.

> You can find a list of recommended reading on my website, www.themunozcompany.com/books.

After many drafts and redrafts, my personal definition of leadership came to be:

> Leadership is to set the course for the organization with ideas that generate from a "good heart," and courageously make the tough yes-or-no decisions, in order to inspire and motivate people to deliver superior results with incredible passion and energy.

The first step in growing your skills as a leader is to define for yourself what you believe good leadership to be. What exactly are you trying to do? How will you know if you are doing well? Consider the following questions, based on an exercise we were assigned at the Academy from the book *In the Arena* by Timothy Quinn:[8]

- Which three leaders would you choose as models? They may be leaders you have known or worked with, leaders you have watched in action, or leaders that you've read about.
- For each person, write down three to five qualities or skills that made you choose them.
- Write a comprehensive definition of leadership (this is a rough draft, so make as many drafts as you like).

---

[8] Timothy G. Quinn and Michelle E. Keith. *In the Arena: Building the Skills for Peak Performance in Leading Schools and Systems*, Old Mission, MI: Quinn and Associates, Ltd., 2010.

- Distill this draft down to a single clear, powerful sentence.

When you're finished, you should be able to identify many different skills you will need to acquire or improve in order to fulfill that definition! As you develop those skills and gain experience, your definition may evolve over time. That's normal. Defining leadership has been a lifelong journey for me. This exercise is a starting point for you to become intentional about the quality of your leadership, and I recommend you return to it periodically throughout your life.

The first step in growing your leadership skills is to define what great leadership means to you.

RESPONSIBILITY AND AUTHORITY

A leader is responsible for moving their organization (or department, or team) toward its ultimate goals. For leaders with total authority, this can be a straightforward matter of issuing directives and holding their team members accountable to follow them. In most situations, however—especially in a school district—the final authority doesn't rest with the leader at all.

A school superintendent is answerable to the board, to the parents, to the labor unions, and often to local elected officials or unofficial power brokers in the community. This requires a different way of leading and a unique set of skills. In addition to your skills in formulating a vision and a personal Theory of Action, you will need skills in building relationships, garnering support, and cultivating influence.

The best advice I can give you on exercising responsibility without authority is to build a strong network of relationships with your stakeholders. In Chapter Four we talked about building relationships on your team—listening and learning, building mutual trust, and protecting them from concerns that they can't help with. You build relationships with your stakeholders the same way.

I would particularly emphasize listening and learning, because it is a broad avenue to build the mutual trust that you need. When your stakeholders have confidence that you are attuned to their needs and concerns, they are more inclined to accept and promote your ideas. Then you must validate their trust by being honest and establishing unshakeable credibility. Stakeholders who trust you but disagree will support you. Those who don't trust you (or who are not trustworthy themselves) can't be relied on for support, even if your plans would benefit them or further their own agenda.

I'd also point out that even leaders with a great deal of authority need to cultivate influence. Authority without positive relationships becomes a kind of dictatorship. A leader who does not listen and learn will lose touch with their own impact on the organization and the community. Wielding authority without accountability or consensus destroys trust. And when a leader can't trust their team, their leadership is doomed. Responsibility transcends authority.

A leader is responsible for delivering results, and responsible to their team and stakeholders.

PREPARING TO LEAD

During my superintendencies, I had many teachers ask me how they could grow into their first administrator role, which is usually either supervisor or vice principal. I would tell them three things: First, excel in your current role. Next, prepare well for the interview. Finally, I'd give them the advice of John Maxwell (and from Acts 20:35) that it's more blessed to give than to receive. In a teaching context that means looking for ways to volunteer for more responsibility, even if it's unpaid. Find groups or projects where you can step up and practice your leadership skills. Will a group follow you if you have no formal authority over them? That's your goal. When administrators see you giving of yourself and improving those skills, and growing, they are more likely to recommend you for future opportunities.

I also had principals and administrators ask my advice on how to advance their careers. They wanted to know everything they would need to do in order to become a director, an assistant supe, or a superintendent. My answer was always the same: the best thing you can do is excel in your current job.

It's good to be ambitious, but I advise you to be cautiously ambitious. Don't be so concerned with your next job that you fail to focus on the work in front of you. This is your opportunity to develop your leadership skills in action, make connections throughout the district, and find mentors who will advocate for you. In some districts (particularly urban districts) it can be hard to find those mentors, but substantive work and a track record of excellence will speak for you.

Indeed, the better your work now, the less heavy lifting advocates will have to do on your behalf. In my experience, it's not unusual for leaders to seek out excellent administrators and invite them to apply for a more senior position based on the quality of the results they're delivering in their role. If you're leading a department, make it a great department. If you're supervising teachers, give useful feedback that will improve the instructional program as a whole. Get your fundamentals right, get your certificates, get your graduate degree, and put all that knowledge into practice. Great leadership has a long learning curve, so the earlier you start the better.

Prepare for a leadership role by leading well in the role you have now.

THE 3 Ss: SCOPE, SEQUENCE, AND SPEED

Mark Zuckerberg famously urged the developers at Facebook to "move fast and break things." Moving from point A to point B is inherently disruptive, but in organizations that serve and value people, an effective leader doesn't seek disruption for its own sake. You aren't trying to create chaos, but to create positive outcomes for your students, your team, and your community. How fast you should move and how many things get "broken" are also referred to as the **3 Ss: Scope**, **Sequence**, and **Speed**. You will be outlining programs, initiatives, and policies that you need to implement. As you design your plan, consider your work in context of the **3 Ss**.

Scope refers to the totality of the work and all its phases. **Sequence** refers to the order in which things need to happen, and whether some changes can happen in parallel. **Speed** is a question of how fast you move through your sequence in order to accomplish the scope. Let's look at how they relate to each other.

The bigger and bolder your scope, the more time you should allow to achieve it. I mentioned in Chapter Three that the changes in my districts felt very fast to the stakeholders because so many of the concepts and strategies I introduced were new. If your stakeholders feel that everything is moving too fast, they may lose confidence in your vision and push back on your ideas. That's where strategic sequencing comes in.

You don't control your speed by slamming on the brakes, but by taking smaller steps. Each incremental change you make should lay the groundwork for the next one. For example, in Chapter Two I described how we changed our math offerings and requirements year by year, so that over three or four years we moved algebra from a ninth-grade expectation to a seventh- and eighth-grade expectation. As your organization sees improvement and success, they will gain confidence in your direction and be more willing to pick up the pace. If your stakeholders think your bold vision is impossible, don't try to accomplish it on Day One, or even Day Ninety. Only take them as far as they will trust you. When you get there, they will be able to see further down the road ahead, so they will trust you more.

YOUR PLAN OF ENTRY

The first ninety days of a superintendent's tenure are very much like the first hundred days of a new presidency. This window is your opportunity to establish the vision and tone of your leadership, make your highest-priority changes, and create momentum and confidence in your organization. You need a clear, written plan of your immediate short-term goals, the actions you'll take to achieve them, and how you'll spend your time.

Your plan should articulate objectives and activities in five major areas: your governance team, organizational capacity and alignment, student achievement, community relations, and operations and finance. Those objectives should always include building relationships and understanding opportunities for improvement—in other words, listening and learning.

> A sample of my Plan of Entry for Passaic can be found in Appendix E.

Those first ninety days can be daunting, because, as the saying goes, you are trying to build the airplane while you're flying it. But remember—you don't have to know everything walking in, and you don't have to do everything all at once. The outcome of your Plan of Entry will be a report back to the school board (and the public) of everything you've learned and how you have incorporated that learning into your vision for the organization and your personal Theory of Action.

If you are still preparing for a leadership role, try creating a ninety day "entry plan" for the job you have today. Consider the different areas of influence your job might intersect with—the team you report to, the team you manage, the students or constituents you ultimately serve, your indirect stakeholders, and your resources. What do you need to learn and understand about those areas? What goals do you want to accomplish in each area for the next three months? What activities should you undertake to reach those goals? Most importantly, how does this short-term plan combine with your personal Theory of Action?

"Start by doing what's necessary, then do what's possible; and suddenly you are doing the impossible."

—ST. FRANCIS OF ASSISI

LEARNING TOGETHER

Professional development is one of the most important vehicles a superintendent can use to change behavior and culture in a school district, and ultimately change outcomes for the students. Good leaders develop talent on their teams; great leaders develop other leaders. You'll recall that in Chapter Four, we discussed the importance of having instructional administrators in your organization who can teach and lead. So, as you grow your leadership skills, you also need to grow your team's skills in those areas. Be intentional about learning as a community of educators.

My three main approaches to professional development were pedagogy and content workshops, a system of interconnected peer study groups I called the Council and Cohorts, and the practice of district-wide instructional rounds. Moreover, I upheld and reinforced high standards for development through regular, rigorous evaluations for staff on every level.

The workshops were quite straightforward—we provided regular opportunities for our classroom teachers to study effective teaching methodologies and master course material. These workshops became more and more important as we shifted the district's programs of study toward rigorous coursework. In Chapter Three, I shared the concept of the instructional core that consists of the teacher, the student, and the content. Our workshops focused on improving the instructional core by increasing the teachers' skills and knowledge of more challenging content, and by improving their teaching methods to maximize student engagement.

COUNCIL AND COHORTS

In his book *Good to Great*,[9] Jim Collins recommends that leaders form an informal strategic thinking group, or council, to help them brainstorm, debate, and understand challenges facing the organization. Members should be drawn from different areas of expertise within the organization, should have equal standing on the council regardless of their job title or seniority, and should be able to advocate a point of view without any self-interest or the desire to win arguments for their own sake.

The makeup of my council was the same, but its purpose was different: to study leadership and build teamwork across disciplines and school assignments, so people from different departments or parts of the district could form bonds and support each other as peers. I assembled a group of about twenty leaders. We all hung our titles outside the door and read books together.

---

9   Jim Collins. Good to Great: *Why Some Companies Make the Leap...and Others Don't*, New York, NY: HarperBusiness, 2001.

Each year we'd select a curriculum of books to study—usually two or three. They might include case studies, business books like *The 5 Levels of Leadership*, *The Five Dysfunctions of a Team*, and *Good to Great*—or they might include texts specifically on educational leadership. We'd meet once a month throughout the year, with assigned reading in between. Each meeting would be led by two members, and at the end of the meeting we'd choose the leaders for next time.

This practice helped us create a common language among key influencers in the district. It allowed members to work on their teaching and leading skills, and it created natural opportunities for members to meet and work closely together who might not cross paths otherwise.

The next stage was to create cohorts. We grouped all the administrators across the district, both instructional and noninstructional, into cross-disciplinary cohorts of fifteen to twenty people. Then two members of the council would lead each cohort in reading and discussing the same material that the council was working on. Including all our administrators in this program demonstrated and reinforced the value we placed on leadership and intentional learning. Sometimes I'd get teased about making such a big deal over "book club," but it was more than worth it to see our administrators grow their leadership skills and relationships.

Lead your team in learning by learning with them.

INSTRUCTIONAL ROUNDS

Back in Chapter Three, I mentioned a text that radically changed my view of professional development: *Instructional Rounds in Education: A Network Approach to Improving Teaching and Learning*.[10] Instructional rounds became the main practice I used to get administrators and teachers to look at instruction objectively, to work through a process of addressing weaknesses in the instructional core in their school, and to identify changes that work. The practice of instructional rounds allows teachers and administrators to systematically visit and observe other schools, help the host principal address problems, and have substantive discussions about what effective instruction really is.

First, we formed networks of administrators and teachers across the district. The networks would meet four or five times a year, rotating through the members' schools. I participated in one network regularly, and as we visited different schools I rotated among the subgroups of my main network. In each school, the host principal would identify a "problem of practice": a specific issue the school was experiencing with some aspect of teaching and learning. For example, are students asking questions, and if not, why not?

The network members would split up into teams, and each team would observe several classrooms. When they reconvened, they presented their observations and discussed how they pertained to the problem at hand. Finally, they made recommendations for how to address the issue and improve instruction in that domain. In our example, the recommendations might include encour-

---

10   Elizabeth A. City, Richard F. Elmore, Sarah E. Fiarman, and Lee Teitel. *Instructional Rounds in Education: A Network Approach to Improving Teaching and Learning*, Cambridge, MA: Harvard Education Press, 2009.

aging students to bring questions to the teacher at any time. Teachers might model productive questions for the class and log the questions that students raised to share with their grade level group. The district might assess whether the curriculum is challenging enough for the students to stay engaged and curious.

This approach has benefits on every level. It is extremely effective at helping the network members develop their professional skills, because they are regularly engaging in thoughtful discussions about teaching and learning, hearing each others' experiences and insights, and considering how to make positive changes. It helps the schools improve instruction for their students with specific recommendations tailored to their needs. And it helps the district identify patterns that may need to be addressed across the system. The district may need to revise certain elements of the organizational Theory of Action policy in order to implement changes at a higher level. Ultimately, instructional rounds helped me instill in my administrators that the core of their jobs is improving teaching and learning. The more they support their teachers' development, the more all the other pieces of the puzzle fall into place.

As much as I believe in and advocate for instructional rounds, they are not the only way to promote learning and teamwork in your district. But no matter what approach you choose, I urge you to be intentional about skill development at every level of your organization. In order to make positive changes, you need all your people rowing in the same direction. This common understanding of teaching and learning, along with your demonstrated investment in raising the bar for everyone, can accelerate culture change and move you toward your ultimate goals that much faster.

Intentional learning accelerates growth.

EVALUATIONS

Testing, adjusting, and public accountability are essential for you to refine your Leader's Algorithm, and they are just as vital to help the administrators and teachers in your district learn and grow. You can leverage the power of feedback through regular evaluations to improve your district's performance in instructional content, pedagogy, and managing and supervising staff.

In low-performing districts, you normally see one of two situations with staff evaluations: either they are not completed at all, or they are only completed in a perfunctory way to comply with state law. They aren't used regularly or effectively to improve teachers' and administrators' performance. The **2 Qs**, **Quality** and **Quantity**, matter when it comes to evaluations.

To the first point, in Passaic there were major problems with the **quantity** of evaluations. In my initial meeting with the incumbent superintendent's cabinet, I asked each person to introduce themselves with their position, length of service, certificates, and the number of staff evaluations they'd done the prior year. When we reached the math supervisor, I asked how many evaluations she did. She just said, "Three."

The room was dead silent. I wasn't sure I heard her correctly, so I thought I'd help her out. "Three a day, three a week, three a month?"

"Three. For the year."

This supervisor had about twenty teachers in her department. By law, tenured teachers had to have two (an annual evaluation plus one more). Nontenured teachers were supposed to have three or four including their annual. Even if every single math teacher were tenured, that's forty evaluations, with 180 days of school to do them in. Clearly, we had an issue.

In Elizabeth, the issue was **quality**. When I was a teacher and administrator, we always complied with the required number of evaluations. However, those evaluations weren't very useful due to a stock phrase: "None at this time."

Our evaluation forms included a rating scale on different aspects of the work, a section to describe the lesson observed, then a section to describe strengths, another to describe areas that needed improvement, and finally a section for advice from the evaluator to the teacher to improve their practice. Evaluators would fill out the top part of the form as needed, but in the section on improvement and advice, they'd always write "None at this time."

Is it any wonder that teaching and learning didn't improve? How can anyone grow their skills if they only receive affirmation for their strengths, but no coaching on their weaknesses?

As a leader, you can apply the **2 Qs** to create enormous leverage for your staff's growth. First, I encourage you to set standards for quantity. The state requirement for evaluations should be a minimum, and as the leader, you should hold your assistant supes, principals, and directors accountable for the number of evaluations their staff receive.

Once you are meeting targets on quantity, it's time to address quality. "None at this time" isn't an acceptable answer. You are responsible for helping your staff grow, and your managers and administrators are responsible for helping their staff grow. Coaching people on ways to improve or giving advice on practice are not inherently negative or critical—that's how you set high expectations and help people achieve them. When the quantity and quality of evaluations come up to an appropriate level, you will see your teachers' and administrators' skills grow by leaps and bounds.

Leverage the power of specific feedback to learn and grow together.

PRACTICE MAKES PROGRESS

Just like ball players need organized, systematic practices to build their skills, educators need planned practice to develop professionally. Collaboration and teamwork help teachers and leaders grow because that supportive community of their peers inspires them and pushes them to study and learn on their own, too. After all, success comes from the practice you do when nobody's looking. As superintendent, you are the chief learner in a community of learners. There is always room to grow, so be intentional about learning with your team—you'll probably wind up learning from your team, too.

Everything you do as a leader, from setting expectations for your district to team building and skill development, depends on buy-in from the community you serve. That's what we'll address in our next chapter, "Leading in Your Community."

CHAPTER 6

LEADING IN YOUR COMMUNITY

"Character is like a tree and reputation its shadow. The shadow is what we think it is, and the tree is the real thing."

—ABRAHAM LINCOLN

Sometimes as a kid, I got to go with my father to work. He was a head chef, serving meals to thousands of people. He ran the kitchen as a tight ship, with an assembly line of plates that had to be filled quickly, precisely, and uniformly. If you've ever been in a commercial kitchen (or watched some of the many reality shows about them), you know that a kitchen has a very clear hierarchy. The head chef has absolute authority, and the dishwasher has none.

I always noticed how my dad (unlike many TV chefs) treated everyone equally. He spoke to everyone respectfully and treated them nicely, regardless of their station in the kitchen or in life. This was an important lesson for me, and I think it's important for anyone in any organization.

The way you treat other people is a matter of character and institutional morale. Beyond that, it's a vital investment in your relationships with the community. Public schools connect in some way or another to nearly every household in a community, and for most families, there are many different points of connection back to that school.

When I was a director of instruction, I met one of our custodians who reminded me so much of my mom. I chatted with her in Spanish, and we regularly took a moment out of our day to greet each other and make conversation. As it happened, she was married to one of our bus drivers. Together, they also ran a small church in the neighborhood. When I became superintendent, it turned out that a number of my school board members attended that same church, and my friend the custodian and her husband were their pastors and spiritual advisors. So all this time, she had been speaking highly of me to her husband, the husband spoke highly of me to their parishioners, and I walked into my position with the board very favorably disposed to my leadership and ideas.

Please don't get me wrong—you should treat everyone equally simply because it's the right thing to do. There is no substitute for sincerity and authenticity. My story is just an example of how doing the right thing can also put you on the right path.

Leadership in your community starts with building relationships. Those bonds give you influence to gather support for your personal Theory of Action. The knowledge you gain and the connections you make will also help you navigate the complex and delicate politics of school leadership.

Treat everyone in your school district and community like your most important stakeholder—because they are.

COMMUNITY RELATIONSHIPS

During your first ninety days, while you're listening and learning to your school board and management team, there is a magic question that can unlock community relationships: "Who else do you think I should speak to?" The answers to that question will give you a wide-ranging list of influential and well-connected people who can give you insight into the school's history, the dynamics of the board, and concerns or challenges outside the school walls that will affect your work inside them.

Community relations or public relations are just broad terms for meeting people who are influential in the community. During my plans of entry, I made a special point of meeting union leaders, elected officials like the mayor and city council, and other community leaders. Sometimes those leaders approached me. Others were suggested by my board members, so I reached out to them. Each of our nine board members gave me at least three names, so I had a list of at least twenty-seven leaders who had significant constituencies in our district. I made a point to meet with each of them and lay the groundwork for open communication.

YOUR LEADERSHIP STORY

We've talked in previous chapters about crafting your personal TOA and your Plan of Entry. Another key document you need to create is your leadership story. You'll be able to use this story in interviews for a leadership position, and when entering a role you should share it with your internal team, your board, and any situation when you're introducing yourself. I waited to include it here because it is so powerful in building positive relationships with members of your community.

Your leadership story lets people understand why you chose the goals and priorities in your Leader's Algorithm, and how you developed as a leader. It tells people who you are, where you came from, your beliefs about education and leadership, and how those beliefs came to be. In a sense, it's your elevator pitch about your experience and vision. It shouldn't just be a summary of your résumé, but really give insight into how you think and operate, and how you envision your leadership style.

Writing your leadership story is another exercise detailed in Tim Quinn's *In the Arena*.[11] I recommend you get a copy for yourself and work through it, but I'll give you a quick overview. Your story should include:

- **Your core values:** Who influenced the formation of your values, and in what way? How do your values inform your work and your life's passion? What common motif links your values to your personal history and work experience?
- **Your strengths as a leader:** Of course you don't want to come across as arrogant, but making an organic connection between your strengths and the rest of your story shows self-awareness and thoughtfulness. How have you used those strengths in service of your values?

---

[11] Timothy G. Quinn and Michelle E. Keith. *In the Arena: Building the Skills for Peak Performance in Leading Schools and Systems*, Old Mission, MI: Quinn and Associates, Ltd., 2010.

- **Your personal influences:** Beyond the formation of your values, what personal relationships have altered the course of your life for the better? How has their influence affected you and your approach to leadership?
- **Your pivot points:** Any good story has twists and turns. Be sure to include moments of realization and decision that changed your perspective on yourself or your course in life.
- **Your future dreams:** Your vision for your current role and how it connects to your values and life's work. What do you want to contribute in this role? How do you want to leave your mark?
- **Your memorable conclusion:** What do you want your audience to take away from this story? What point do you want them to remember most?

You should prepare longer and shorter versions of your story for different contexts. If you have ten or fifteen minutes to address a town hall forum, you'll be more comprehensive. If you're sitting down for coffee with a neighborhood leader, you need a brief introduction that doesn't dominate the conversation. Once you capture the core elements of your story, you can tailor it to any situation.

Understand your own leadership story so you can share it with others.

BONDS OF TRUST

A great example of the importance of community relationships was my connection with a local pastor. Like many community leaders, he wanted to know he had access to me if he ever needed it. He considered his relationships with other community figures to be part of his role as the leader of his organization—just like me.

As we chatted, I got to know a little about him. He grew up and went to high school in the area. One of his members turned out to be a colleague. It was a lovely conversation. We exchanged numbers. He said, "Listen, I just want to be able to pick up the phone and talk to you if I need your help with one of my parishioners."

I agreed, and periodically throughout my tenure, that's exactly what he would do. I'd try to help with any problem he brought to me, and if I couldn't, I'd explain why. The one problem I couldn't solve for him hit right at home: a relative of his worked in the district as a principal. For a number of reasons, we didn't renew the principal's contract.

Now, in New Jersey, the superintendent has final say on employee renewal. If they decide not to renew someone, they don't need board approval. However, if the employee petitions the board, the board could vote to renew them for next year.

This principal didn't want to go back to being a vice principal. The story got into the press "somehow," and there was a big story that emphasized how much the principal was loved. Of course, I always discussed everything with my board, so I already knew that I had their agreement on the matter. Nevertheless, my friend, the pastor, called me on the day of the board meeting. He was up front about the fact that this principal was a family member, and told me he was getting calls about the nonrenewal. He told me he was hearing different stories about the possible reasons behind it. He asked me what was going on and whether I could intervene.

I was as transparent as I could be with him. I shared that the principal's contract had already been extended once, but that the principal could not continue in the position. I may have been more transparent than I should have, but in a situation like that you have to get your point across. I needed him to understand that this decision wasn't taken lightly and there was nothing shady or untoward about it.

He and I both knew that, had he chosen to do so, he could have mobilized a large and vocal congregation—and everyone they were connected to—to oppose me. He could have made my job untenable and my life a misery. Instead, he listened. He understood. He trusted me.

He knew that everything I had said since we first met had been honest and borne out in fact. Everything I had told him I would do, I did. Any help I could give him, I gave. So when I had to say, "No, the school needs someone else in that position," he trusted that I had good reasons for it.

Can you imagine how differently that conversation could have gone if there were no history of mutual trust between us? Instead of, "Hey, what's really going on here?" it might have been, "Explain yourself!" Instead of, "Is there anything you can do?" it could have been, "How dare you!" That initial investment of listening and learning, compounded with time and cooperation, paid dividends in a strong tie of mutual respect.

Transparency and integrity create solid community relationships.

PUBLIC RELATIONS AND THE PRESS

There's an adage in the advertising business: "Sell the sizzle, not the steak." You can tell people all day about how tasty your steak will be, but they won't buy it. Hearing that steak sizzle makes their mouths water. Suddenly, they can imagine how delicious that steak will be. They get excited about it. They want it, right now.

As we discussed in Chapter Three, people need emotional reasons to buy into your ideas, rather than logical ones. For most people, logic moves them to contemplation. Emotions move them to action.

In both Elizabeth and Passaic, our sizzle was the high school transformation initiative. It was a big, dramatic change. We could boil it down to a simple pitch, brand it with a catchy name, and make a splashy announcement. We mailed out newsletters to every household in the district. We interviewed principals to see which school would be the best fit. We talked and wrote about it constantly as part of our mission and vision. The headlines were easy to write, and we got them.

Here's the problem: if you sell the sizzle and never deliver the steak, or the steak turns out to stink, you lose all that support. People will feel cheated. They trusted you, and you let them down. So as a superintendent, you must be mindful of both: sell the sizzle, and deliver the steak.

When it comes to turning around an underperforming district, the steak is the instructional core. Announcing our high school initiatives bought us support and time, because we had a long way to go academically. Dividing up the students into new buildings and slapping a bunch of new names on things wasn't going to transform their academic outcomes overnight. If we didn't follow through, it would just be like rearranging deck chairs on the *Titanic*. We had to show up every day and deliver the steak of teaching and learning. We had to ensure the quality of the steak through continuous improvement to our practices. We couldn't let our steak stink. We had to keep our promise, and make it great.

While I was in transition from Elizabeth to Passaic, a reporter called me for an interview. He asked what I considered my greatest accomplishment in Elizabeth. Was it the six new high schools? Was it our state and national rankings? Was it making the *US News & World Report* lists?

I told him, "No. It's not any of those things. This isn't sexy and it won't make good copy for you, but here's the truth: my greatest accomplishment is that my students are performing better academically, taking more Advanced Placement courses, and getting into better colleges than when I started."

Now, that's quality steak.

Sell the sizzle, and deliver the steak.

ADDRESS COMMUNITY NEEDS

There's another aspect to forming good relationships with your community through public relations—making sure the community hears and reads about the ways that you are addressing their concerns. Most parents and residents in a school district will never have occasion to talk directly with the superintendent. Their confidence in the organization's direction (or lack thereof) is shaped by student and family experiences, community influencers, and especially by what they read and see in the press and on social media. They need to know that school leadership understands their needs, has priorities aligned with their own, and is taking constructive action to address them. As we discussed in Chapter One, making your personal Theory of Action a public document helps the community understand your priorities, plans, and philosophy. You can boost awareness of your improvements and accomplishments by sharing positive stories with the media.

At The Broad Academy, we had a very helpful module on public relations. Our instructor pointed out that parents and the community care about three things, in this order:

1. The safety and security of their children;
2. Their children's academic achievement;
3. Whether their tax dollars are being spent efficiently and wisely.

Don't wait for the local newspaper, TV station, or social media outlet to come to you asking questions. By the time that happens, you'll be doing damage control for some kind of complaint or negative story. Instead, engage proactively with the media by crafting press releases that highlight one of these touchpoints. If a press release is well written, a local paper will often simply reprint it. By providing positive stories on the issues that matter most, you can let the community know that you are in tune with their biggest concerns and taking practical steps to address them.

Engage the public in your successes by speaking to their interests.

INFLUENCE AND PERSUASION

When it comes to your relationship with your school board, local government, and your community, context matters. The location and environment of your district will determine how much you depend on community input to accomplish the goals in your personal Theory of Action. I've had colleagues working in the suburbs who needed twenty different town hall meetings in order to make a single policy change. I felt fortunate in my two urban districts that I only had to convince my board to support a proposal, and it was done. Indeed, for most of my tenures in Elizabeth and Passaic, I had one key board member that I really needed to present my ideas to. Once they bought into a plan, they could bring the rest of the board with them. Leaders aren't always so lucky. Whether the board aligns with you easily or not, it's a good idea to meet with every board member regularly (even the ones you struggle to get along with). Constant investment into those relationships builds your influence by building trust.

When disagreement or misalignments arise, it's very important that you and your board present a united front. Make a habit of holding informal or partial meetings before the official meeting, so you can understand your stakeholders' concerns and hash out disagreements privately. You don't want to be put on the spot or make anyone else look bad in the glare of a public meeting. If your board members need detailed answers, informal discussions give you a chance to gather information and address those concerns comprehensively.

Leadership is relational, not positional. You may find that one or more board members holds an outsized influence over the others, regardless of their title. Some boards rotate their officers on a regular basis to distribute the workload, so this year's president may have much less sway than a member at large. Meeting with board members in small groups or committees gives you a chance to feel out which way the vote may go on a controversial topic, and which members align with different positions. I never went into an official board meeting without knowing which way the vote would go, and I didn't bring any proposal up for a vote unless I knew it would pass.

The same holds true for labor unions, administrators, the city council, or any group of stakeholders that needs to officially endorse your proposals in order to proceed. Make sure you have thoroughly discussed the issue with the leaders and influencers of that group and addressed their concerns. Making sure you have alignment lets you move forward with confidence instead of getting bogged down in controversy.

Debate in private so you can be unified in public.

THE 2X2 MATRIX

When I first became a superintendent, a friend told me that there's not a problem in the world that can't be solved with a 2x2 matrix. At first I laughed, but over time—darned if he isn't right. This little matrix leads to powerful conversations and provides a framework for the most change-intensive initiatives.

The 2x2 matrix is a mental model that illustrates how I approach leadership and decision-making. It's a way to simplify the many demands of the stakeholders in a school district and understand that education happens inside the context of a political system. Whenever I had to make recommendations about policy, personnel, programs, facilities, budget, or any other aspect of my work in the district, I would think through what I needed to say and how to approach it using the 2x2 matrix.

You may be familiar with this decision-making tool as a way to present options and variables. When your organization needs to balance two conflicting values, this diagram brings focus and clarity to the outcomes of prioritizing one value over another. For example, in *The 7 Habits of Highly Effective People*, Stephen Covey puts urgency on one axis and importance on the other.[12] All the different tasks you might work on can be assigned to one of the four quadrants, to help you determine the most valuable use of your time.

In my 2x2 matrix, I place student achievement on one axis and political demands on the other. Each quadrant has a different relative priority, and a different outcome.

---

[12] Stephen R. Covey. *The 7 Habits of Highly Effective People*, New York, NY: Simon & Schuster, 1989.

Students & Politics Matrix

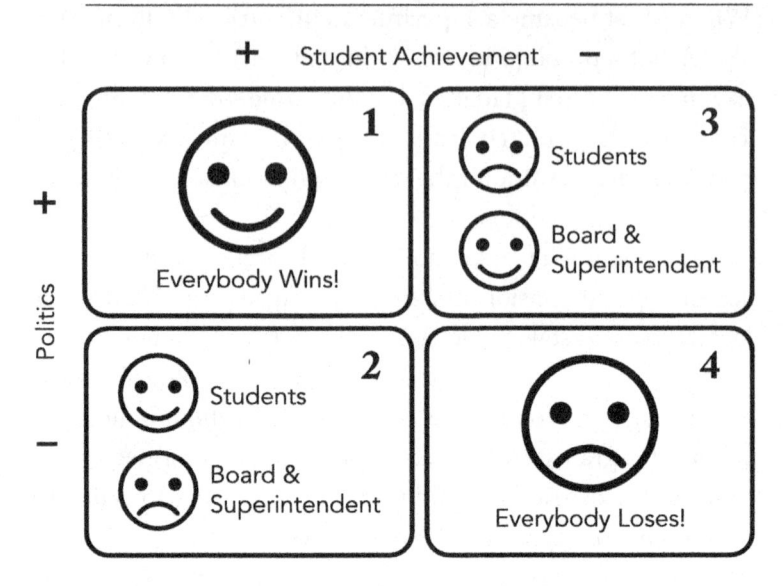

Student Achievement (+ to −)

Politics (+ to −)

Quadrant 1 (+Politics, +Achievement): 😊 Everybody Wins!

Quadrant 2 (−Politics, +Achievement): 🙂 Students / ☹ Board & Superintendent

Quadrant 3 (+Politics, −Achievement): ☹ Students / 🙂 Board & Superintendent

Quadrant 4 (−Politics, −Achievement): ☹ Everybody Loses!

Copyright 2022 by Pablo Muñoz. All Rights Reserved.

- In Quadrant 1, we get our political influencers on board with ideas that promote student achievement. As a result, the students are learning at higher levels because of our work. The students and parents are happy. The school board and other elected officials are happy because they get high public approval ratings. We get to continue building a better student experience. Everyone wins.
- In Quadrant 2, we make decisions to promote student achievement, but not all of our political stakeholders are persuaded to support them. There is significant resistance, and we are in an uphill battle. Our students are achieving at higher levels, and their parents are happy, but there is a political cost. Every move we make will be scrutinized, and eventually we may find ourselves forced to choose between difficult concessions or losing our jobs.

- In Quadrant 3, we are fully invested in playing politics without regard to student achievement. The political influencers are appeased, but there is no accountability, and no clear expectations or systems to support academic success. Student achievement has plateaued or even declined, but our political stakeholders are happy.
- In Quadrant 4, everyone is miserable. Student learning is declining, we fail in our mandate to improve academic performance, the political influencers are receiving public criticism, and we're all likely to lose our jobs.

> You can download a blank template for the 2x2 matrix from my website, **www.themunozcompany.com**.

Naturally, everyone wants to be in Quadrant 1 all the time. Everyone likes a win–win situation. But life isn't a static diagram. Circumstances are constantly changing. You could be working happily in Quadrant 1, a new slate of members is elected to the board, and some of them vehemently disagree with your ideas. Boom, all of a sudden you're in Quadrant 2. By the same token, a superintendent can't hang out in Quadrant 3 forever. A political superintendent who is very good at horse-trading can keep a district stagnant for a long time, but if there is no accountability for results, they will eventually devolve into Quadrant 4: achievement bottoms out, the public gets fed up, or the state will step in with new mandates, and there's a shake-up.

Your job as a leader is to lead change and improvement, so think of this matrix like a chessboard. No matter where you start, your goal is to wind up in Quadrant 1 as much as possible. Sometimes it may take a couple of moves to get there.

Let me give you a real-world example. We needed to appoint a new principal for a school, and it turned into a political battle. There were two candidates, both vice principals, and I'll refer to them as A and B.

Candidate A had been a teacher in the district for many years before being promoted to vice principal. She was dedicated to teaching and learning, and was a very competent administrator. She was humble and focused on her students. I knew she could do a great job with that particular school.

Candidate B was a vice principal and very well-connected with some of the school board members. He had good qualifications on paper and a good track record as a manager. But he was arrogant, and he didn't have teaching and learning as his top priority. (There's also the fact that he forgot to update his cover letter, so he accidentally sang the praises of another district he was applying to.)

I favored Candidate A. The board president and some of his allies favored candidate B. Suddenly, I had to choose my starting position on the 2x2 matrix. Would I take the path of least resistance into Quadrant 3 and go along with the board president? Or would I push for my own choice in the face of political resistance and jump into Quadrant 2? Either way, how could I work my way back to Quadrant 1?

Well, my personal TOA and our organizational TOA are focused on student achievement, so it really wasn't much of a choice. I started counting votes. We had a nine-member school board. Our board president and three other members wanted Candidate B, along with a couple of highly placed city officials. Those officials were influential, but they didn't have a vote. So that was four votes for Candidate B, with five to play for.

I knew that my two strongest allies on the board held sway over the other three, so I connected with them to let them know how strongly I felt about the issue, and why. As usual, we held a private session before the public session, and I recommended Candidate A based on her strength as an instructional leader. I put all my cards on the table, and then my two strongest allies took the floor. They challenged the other board members to give a good reason why they would ignore my recommendation. They wound up being even more persuasive than I had hoped, because not only did I carry the vote with my five allies, one of Candidate B's supporters changed their mind and voted with me. Candidate A was approved, six to three.

Interestingly, the public vote to appoint Candidate A was unanimous. The school board members were all part of the same local political party, and to have a split vote in public would have been embarrassing. Eventually, even those three board members who voted to save face came around. After the new principal had the chance to actualize her leadership and the school flourished, it was obvious she had been the right choice all along. In the end, we all wound up in Quadrant 1 together.

Whenever you need to check your priorities and make a decision with a group, the 2x2 matrix is an amazing tool. It helps you focus on what is most important and make decisions that will best implement your personal Theory of Action.

The 2x2 matrix brings clarity and focus to complex decisions.

NAVIGATING POLITICS

My mentor and advocate Rafael Fajardo taught me a lot about politics. Rafael served on the Elizabeth school board for decades, and was very aware of the games some people play in the public school system. From time to time when people would approach him to chat, he'd turn to me and say, *"Ese huevo quiere sal."*

"That egg wants salt." It's a Cuban expression indicating that someone has an ulterior motive. Many people within the school organization try to leverage relationships with politicians for their personal advancement, and vice versa. I was pretty clueless about political machinations during my career as a teacher and administrator. Becoming superintendent was a wake-up call.

You often have to read between the lines with your board and elected officials. Sometimes people will say one thing in public and something different to you in private. Sometimes they whisper a comment as if it's a secret between you and then go out and do the opposite of what you expected. Unfortunately, I've come to realize that people lie a lot.

Headlines can lie, too—certainly, they can give a distorted picture of events. Ethical reporters try to make sure their stories are corroborated with artifacts and evidence beyond the shifting tales that people tell, but even the best reporter can only get so close to a story. And even when everyone involved has the purest of intentions, people see things differently and have unreliable memories. All those factors can add up to a lot of negative attention and grief for school leaders.

The last thing you want is for fear of negative publicity or political blowback to hamper your effectiveness as a leader. Yet that fear is real. I've fallen into it myself in the past, and my leadership suffered for it. Your security as a leader comes back to understanding and strengthening relationships with other leaders in your district.

POLITICAL MAPPING

As you create your lists of community leaders to connect with, it behooves you to keep track of the constituency that each person can bring to the table. Every local politician and community leader has a certain area of influence, whether it springs from neighborhood geography, political party, religious affiliation, business interests, or anything else. You need to understand how different leaders can help improve the schools and move you toward your ultimate goal, or create obstacles that could derail you. More importantly, you need to understand (as best you can) their goals and why they might oppose your ideas.

Nobody is going to say that they are against improving education. But they may have different priorities, a favored candidate, or an ideological agenda that conflicts with your plans. A clear mental (or literal) map of the circles of influence in your community can help you find your strongest supporters. It can also alert you when you need to change your position in the 2x2 matrix. You might not be able to stay in Quadrant 1 where everyone is happy. From time to time you might need to step into Quadrant 2 and push for your goals despite political resistance.

Public school politics can be treacherous waters. You need a clear map of allies and obstacles to help you navigate.

LEVERAGE

Sometimes you simply can't persuade a key figure to support your initiatives, no matter how much listening and trust-building you do, and no matter how much you try to address their concerns. Some people hold views that can't be reconciled with your own. Some people just won't like you. In a case like that, the best course is to step back and let someone else persuade them for you.

In Chapter Three I described my bold dream in Passaic to eliminate the middle school and fold those grades into K–8, 6–12, and 9–12 campuses. I was able to bring the board around to my thinking, but there was a key stakeholder in the community who wouldn't even entertain the notion: the mayor. Now, we'd been working on this proposal for several years. We'd been through four different board presidents, and the town had a different mayor than the one we'd initially briefed on the plan.

As we got closer to taking the full vote of the board to approve the plan, the new board president decided to reopen discussions with the mayor's office. Suddenly, we had a problem. The mayor (for the sake of some idea of his own) couldn't get on board with combining middle schoolers and elementary school students in the same building. We discussed placing grades 6–12 together, and he wouldn't support that either. I'm still not sure what issue he had with the idea, but he was adamant that this would be unwelcome to parents and disruptive to the community.

Nothing could have been further from the truth. Passaic is a geographically small, dense city. None of our students lived more than two miles from their school, so we only provided bussing for students with medical needs or special circumstances. It's also a poor community, so most families were not dropping their kids off in the carpool. We had a lot of walkers, and a lot of larger families with kids in multiple schools. A family with a prekindergartener, a second-grader, a sixth-grader, and a high schooler would have kids in four different schools.

Consolidating a K–8 school would be a godsend. The parents were thrilled to hear it. It would simplify their lives so much to only have to go to one neighborhood school, and then only deal with one transition to high school. But the mayor would not acknowledge that his views were out of touch with the community's needs and interests.

The boost we needed for the program came, somewhat unexpectedly, from the police department. The district had an excellent relationship with the police because we had school resource officers working in our schools all day, and my security supervisor was the former chief of police. When the police department heard about the K–8 plan, they leaped to support it.

In our original school configuration, there was one large middle school in the center of town. Every morning and every afternoon, they had 1,800 seventh- and eighth-graders from all over the city swarming in and out of that small area. There was always trouble. It was a huge headache for the police to keep order and monitor the foot traffic from all those pent-up adolescents hitting the streets at the same time.

Under the new plan, those students were dispersed to neighborhood schools all over town instead of being concentrated in one place. It's been my experience that in a K–8 or pre-K–8 scenario, the middle schoolers respond positively to the presence of the younger kids. Many of them are older siblings of the young students, and they all have a tendency to assume that big-brother, big-sister role. These schools naturally create positive dynamics in the community, instead of the isolated middle school creating a *Lord of the Flies* scenario every day.

Announcing our plans and bringing the police department into discussions about them was one of the best moves we could have made. In the end, we didn't have to persuade the mayor at all. The parents and his own police department persuaded him for us. And after the reorganization was complete, if you visited the city center at school dismissal time you could hear a pin drop.

Leverage your allies to persuade people for you.

NEGOTIATION

Whether your relationships with your school board are warm and supportive or political and transactional, you will have to deal with contracts, budgeting, and allocating finite resources. That means you need to negotiate. Keep in mind what you really want and need in order to carry out your personal TOA, and put those goals first in every planning discussion.

As I mentioned in our discussion of the 2x2 matrix, you have to navigate whatever circumstances come your way. There isn't always a direct path from Quadrant 2 or 3 back to Quadrant 1. Sometimes your board will feel very strongly about a decision (like a personnel issue), and you simply can't get the votes to carry the day. If you know you can't make headway, don't make waves. Wait for the waters to calm down and see how you can do the most good for your students in the long run.

If you antagonize a majority of the board over a single appointment, that could lock you into Quadrant 2 or 4 for a long time. It could hold up your whole agenda—policies, programs, initiatives, and all the other changes you're trying to make. It's better to take a political appointee in Quadrant 3 than to bog down everything else you're trying to accomplish. And after all, if you continue to work on building strong relationships and investing in your team to help them grow, that political appointee may come around and be a great team member.

Take the long view. There will always be vacancies somewhere in a district. People retire. They resign. They get promoted. If you're making systemic changes, you might need to staff up new schools. There will always be opportunities to place the candidates you want in key positions, sooner or later.

Create a package deal for yourself, but don't refer to it that way. Simply offer your board a slate of candidates that includes their favored pick, along with your choice of candidates for three, four, or five other positions. The longer you stay in your leadership position, the more you invest in your team, the better candidates you'll have for internal promotions. These proven assets will make it even easier for the board to endorse your picks. For the sake of one less-than-ideal political appointee, you could get a whole group of excellent team members. In the end, you'll be gaining more than you lose, and have that much more momentum toward your ultimate goal.

I don't like working in the transactional mindset of Quadrant 3, and I don't recommend it as a general rule. But if you find yourself in a corner and horse-trading is your best option, just make sure you come out on the better end of the deal—and make sure your decisions will yield positive results for the students in the long run.

Always negotiate package deals, so that a compromise on details doesn't compromise your vision, mission, and goals.

No matter what political difficulties you may face, remember that your first duty is to improve your students' educational outcomes. You may need to compartmentalize your discussions with your closest advisors, so that political friction doesn't spill over onto your main business. Keep your focus—and your organization's focus—on teaching and learning. That's what you're there for.

Your consistent and persistent focus on quality education demonstrates your credibility and integrity to everyone you deal with. Your Leader's Algorithm invites them to hold you accountable. The trust you build with your stakeholders strengthens your influence in the community, and your ability to achieve your goals.

Leadership in a community means understanding their goals and serving their needs. Sometimes those needs can be overwhelming. Stresses and demands from the community, from your team, and from your life can sometimes knock you off balance or wear you down over time. You need to find support and consciously practice resilience, so you can weather all the storms you face. That's our topic in Chapter Seven, "Leading with Resilience."

CHAPTER 7

LEADING WITH RESILIENCE

"Our greatest glory is not in never falling, but in rising every time we fall."

—CONFUCIUS

Long before I started as superintendent in Elizabeth, there was a political war going on among the school board, the mayor, and the state senator for the district. It was a blood sport, and I was caught in the crossfire. In 2006, the dispute erupted into a lawsuit by the board against the city. This was followed by intense scrutiny from state regulators and repeated official audits of the school system's finances, which many believed to be harassment and retaliation by the senator. I did my best to push through the noise and get on with the job.

The ongoing conflict led to investigative reports by the local newspapers. Those articles induced the state attorney general's office to get involved. The attorney general uncovered real scandals and malfeasance, leading to criminal investigations of some key people in the district hierarchy. In the fall of 2011, the situation came to a head. Subpoenas were flying, charges were brought, and I wound up having to get a criminal defense attorney, just to be on the safe side. I tried to keep my head down and keep on pushing through.

The job of superintendent is stressful enough in ordinary times. This minefield of conflict, accusations, secrets, and betrayal was intolerable. I have had anxiety my whole life, and periods of intense stress have from time to time brought on major depressive episodes. As the pressures around me escalated, it happened again.

The first symptom I noticed was that I stopped watching football games on Sunday. I knew the Jets would be a disappointment and I'd be bummed out. That doesn't sound like much, but sports are such a big part of my life that this was a huge change. I was losing interest in things I loved, but the only words I could use to describe it were "bummed out."

I felt sad and flat. I cried often. I was anxious and my mind was in an unrelenting fog. I wasn't sleeping. I wasn't eating. I lost a lot of weight. I looked so ill, people started to pull me aside and ask if I was all right.

I was not. I kept pushing through anyway.

By December of 2011, I couldn't push through anymore. We were spending Christmas break at our vacation home on the Jersey shore, and I had a ministroke (a transient ischemic attack). I wound up in the hospital. The doctors got me fixed up with cholesterol medicine, blood thinners, and vitamin D, but we didn't address my mental health at all.

When I went back to work, my physical state just made everything worse. I found a therapist and started medication, but it wasn't helping very much. People tried to reassure me that everything would be all right, but that didn't help either—particularly when the school board's attorney (the very person who tried the hardest to calm me down) was arrested and charged.

I was continuing to manage the district. In fact, we were still improving and won National Blue Ribbon awards. I was contacted by several other districts that wanted to recruit me. And still the chaos and battles went on.

By the spring of 2012, it was all just too much. I called my counselor in tears one morning and said, "I can't handle it anymore." She told me to get to the hospital right away.

I checked myself in for intensive inpatient care and spent three weeks in the psychiatric ward. It was exactly where I needed to be, because the doctors can adjust your medication every day if they need to, and fine-tune the care you need. I went to group therapy every day. I started eating again. I also met other patients with fascinating personal stories. Altogether, it was a very positive experience for me.

Gradually I transitioned to outpatient care with regular therapy and medication. I was able to sleep and function. Districts were still recruiting me, and later that year I applied to Passaic. It was still a high-pressure job, but a completely different and happier environment, which made all the difference.

I had spent years cultivating my educational skills and leadership skills, but I hadn't invested at all in my emotional health or my support network. I thought that having integrity and a strong character were enough to see me through. They weren't. They aren't.

The thing is, I was struggling for a long time before it started to show on my face. I had always prided myself on staying calm and collected in high-pressure situations. From the pitcher's mound as a kid, to high-stakes conflicts at home or at work, I always felt like a duck on the water: looking serene, but paddling furiously underneath.

> If you're in crisis, don't wait. Call or text "**988**" to reach the national Suicide and Crisis Lifeline. They will connect you to trained counselors who will listen, understand how your problems are affecting you, provide support, and connect you to resources if necessary. You can also connect by live chat at their website, **www.988lifeline.org**.

I learned a number of lessons from that experience, as well as other experiences throughout my career that these events made me see in a new light. I want to share those lessons with you, so you can become resilient and weather the inevitable storms of leadership.

The most important lesson was that I needed help, and I should have had it years earlier. Instead, I tried to suck it up and carry on as if nothing were wrong. *It broke me.* Don't make the same mistake.

Looking okay is not the same as being okay; ask for help before you're forced to.

STAYING CENTERED

The political fight between the school board and the state senator wasn't my fight. It had been going on before I was involved, and it kept going on after I left. Nevertheless, I wound up in the middle of it because I was the board's preferred candidate for the superintendency, so I was "their guy." I accepted that position and ran with it.

On the face of things, it appeared to me that the board's motivation was to pursue academic excellence for the district. That was my passion as well, so we had a natural alignment. I was so focused on that goal that I didn't realize there were many layers to the political conflict, and many risks to getting involved in it. Unfortunately, I drew the wrath of the politicians on the other side of that conflict by making some negative public comments about them.

I didn't realize how powerful some elected officials can be, or how vindictive they can be if you attract their attention in a negative way. Politics is a game of connections. As much as I work on making positive connections with the community, my connections are no match for a successful incumbent in public office. A couple of well-placed phone calls, and they were able to sic the New Jersey Department of Education and the US Department of Justice on us. This taught me an important lesson about concern and influence.

In *The 7 Habits of Highly Effective People*, Stephen Covey discusses the relationship between your Circle of Concern and your Circle of Influence.[13] They are depicted as concentric cir-

---

[13] Stephen R. Covey. *The 7 Habits of Highly Effective People*, New York, NY: Simon & Schuster, 1989.

cles. The outer circle, your Circle of Concern, encompasses everything in life that you *care about*, which includes things that affect you directly as well as things that matter to you emotionally or indirectly. The inner circle, your Circle of Influence, is smaller. It only includes the things you can directly or indirectly *change*—your impact on the world. Within that inner circle, you can make a difference. In the outer circle, you have concern but no influence.

Of course, we all care about things that we can't control, from the weather or the health of our loved ones to famine or wars happening on the other side of the world. But the more time and energy we spend outside our Circle of Influence, the more helpless and anxious we feel. We are more inclined to lash out or denigrate others, because we feel as if our words are the only tool we have. Even worse, the more time we spend outside our Circle of Influence, the smaller it gets. We become unproductive and ineffective. We withdraw from people (or actively alienate them). Placing our center of focus outside our Circle of Influence becomes a vicious cycle—our worries grow and our agency shrinks, making our zone of "concern without influence" bigger and bigger.

Instead, Covey advises spending most of our time and effort inside our Circle of Influence. That doesn't mean ignoring current events or just keeping your head down to endure a bad situation! Think about all the things that are inside your Circle of Influence: your physical and mental health; your network of personal and professional support; your relationships with your staff, mentors, students, and parents; your family and friends; your civic duties; your charitable giving or volunteer work; and so much more.

All these aspects of your life need your intentional investment of time and attention. They must be cultivated. If you ignore them, they suffer. As you nurture them, they flourish. Those thriving connections and self-care make you more resilient. Even better, when you spend time and energy inside your Circle of Influence, it grows. The more you work on making a difference where you can, the more difference you're able to make.

In my second superintendency I kept my mouth shut about local politics. I understood that there is always more going on than you realize. Airing negative opinions isn't going to achieve anything positive. In order to pursue your vision and reach the ultimate goal of your personal Theory of Action, you need unity and cooperation from the whole community—those you agree with and those you don't. Make a positive impact with your words and actions.

Build your resilience by building positive connections and taking positive action in your personal life and your work.

CREATING BALANCE

The leader's role can be all-consuming. You're on call twenty-four hours a day, and if you're not careful, that can easily turn into being on the clock 24/7. That's not a sustainable way to live. It disrupts your family, weakens your personal relationships, and wears you out. You need to create boundaries around your time and attention, so you can balance your work with your health and the rest of your life.

Let's look again at your personal Theory of Action. Your first line item is all about focus. Your second is about selecting leaders.

If you're tempted to stay overconnected and overcommitted, the first thing to examine is your team. Whether you call them your cabinet or your executive team, these are the people you should be delegating to. In my superintendencies, I was very careful to choose assistant supes, business administrators, and a chief of operations who were very strong in their roles. I'd fight my school board to get the right people if I had to. They needed to be very smart and, frankly, better than me in their respective areas.

Knowing that you have the best possible person in each key role will allow you to step back and let them carry their share of the load without micromanaging. In fact, you are doing them a disservice if you don't delegate to them and let them get on with their jobs. They need a level of autonomy and authority in order to develop their own leadership skills.

Next, enforce some space and distance in communication. I started as a superintendent before smartphones came out, but when they did, I loved mine. I got my calendar and my school email set up on my phone, so I could be reached anywhere, anytime, by anyone.

That wasn't good! I began having problems at home because I was constantly on my phone, reading and dealing with work emails when I was supposed to be relaxing or spending time with family. It certainly didn't help my stress levels.

Things got much better when I deleted my work email from

my phone altogether. If anyone really needed to reach me after hours, they could go through other channels. If the matter truly needed my attention, someone in the chain of command would call me. There were several times when that happened—pipes bursting in a school building, for example. I was always ready to go back into the office if necessary, but allowing the chain of command to act as a filter restored a level of sanity in my home. It also improved my relationships with my cabinet. Deleting the email stopped me from hovering and interfering in minor issues that I didn't need to worry about.

When you have leaders working under you that you trust, and you have boundaries on your communication, then you can begin to effectively implement boundaries on your time.

Create balance in your life by hiring leaders you can trust.

BE A PLOW HORSE, NOT A SHOW HORSE

After my hospitalization, I got very clear on my priorities and became selective about how I spent my time, especially time outside regular office hours. From time to time, I would get criticism from school board members who wanted to see me attend more community events in the evenings and on weekends. I know that some people see great value in making all sorts of public appearances. I don't.

I was brought into those school districts for a very specific purpose: to improve academic performance. My focus was on improving the instructional core, and that happens inside the classroom, in the relationship between the teacher, the student, and the content. It doesn't occur at a basketball game or a community prayer service. It's very important to make connections with community members, but in order to make authentic connections you need to *talk* with people one-on-one or in small groups. Simply being seen in a crowd or shaking a bunch of hands has no benefit in itself.

When my own children were younger, I spent more time out and about with them in Elizabeth. They're athletes, so I wound up attending a lot of games. As they transitioned to high school and college and played on travel teams, our lifestyle revolved around four- or five-hour drives to games every weekend. I simply couldn't be everywhere at once.

Going back to my personal Theory of Action, I had to consider what actions would produce my desired results. At work, I wanted to see results in academic excellence, and in my own life I wanted to see better health, better sleep, and more time with my family. Would making a token appearance at public events produce those results? Not likely.

When board members in Passaic got upset with me for not attending as many events as they'd like, we had to have a talk. I explained to them that if they wanted to hire a show horse to go out and do meet and greets all the time, they got the wrong guy. I'm a plow horse. My priorities were to take care of my family and add value to our students' learning. Anything that would take time away from one or the other was off the table, period.

You will always encounter a few people who want to set your

priorities for you, but a good leader can't afford to be a people pleaser. I once heard another superintendent say, "I give blood every day at work. I need to keep some for myself."

That's absolutely right. Make your own decisions about how best to use your limited time and energy. Stay focused on your vision and your ultimate goal, and don't let other people fill up your to-do list with their own preferences.

Never sacrifice results for appearances.

FIND YOUR ADVOCATES

At every stage of my career I had an advocate. I first became a teacher because Herb Hennessy, the supervisor of social studies in the New Haven public schools, did a campus crawl at Yale and sat down with me at lunch to ask about my future. He introduced me to Edith MacMullin, the professor in charge of the teacher preparation program at Yale. Between the two of them, they ignited my passion for teaching and helped me all along the way. Edith also prepared dossiers for all her student teachers to help them find work, so when my hometown district decided to recruit, I was ready.

Then the director of human resources in Elizabeth, Tom Ficarra, took an interest in me and gave me stretch assignments to develop my leadership skills. Over the summers, he kept me busy working on new teacher handbooks. He took me on a recruiting trip back to Yale. He advised me to go back to graduate school to prepare to be an administrator.

Ray Korn, my high school baseball coach, was still in Elizabeth, too. He wanted me to join his coaching squad. He networked with the local college to get me a position there as pitching coach, and later he introduced me to the Chicago Cubs recruiters, who hired me as a minor-league pitching coach. All of these experiences helped to shape my understanding of leadership.

The list of people who advocated for me throughout my career would take up a book on its own. Every step of the way, someone helped me up, gave me chances, made the right introductions, or gave me good advice. These people weren't merely useful stepping stones in my career advancement. They helped me develop as an educator, a leader, and a human being. They supported and encouraged me. They guided me in the right direction. They cheered me on. They cared about me.

It is so important for a leader to realize that you can't accomplish anything alone. You need your team to execute your personal TOA, but you also need advocates who go ahead of you and mentors who walk beside you. You need to lean on people, ask questions, follow opportunities, and learn from their experience. And precisely because you can't do it alone, that also means *you aren't alone.* Your network of advocates can be a source of strength and resilience when you need it most.

When you need courage, help, or support, remember all the people who encouraged and supported you along the way.

RESILIENT LEADERSHIP

There were many differences in tone and context between the communities of Elizabeth and Passaic. Though Passaic had less chaos and conflict, it was still a demanding, stressful role. That's just the nature of the job. However, I went into the new position much better equipped to reduce stressors where I could and to cope with the rest.

I had professional counseling and well-adjusted brain chemistry, for starters. Beyond that, I had more skills and self-knowledge to manage stressful situations in a constructive way. And I had more resources to draw on, because I had identified specific people I could call on or actions I could take to recover and bounce back from stress.

Planning for resilience is a lot like writing a personal TOA, starting from the bottom line up. If your ultimate goal is mental and emotional health, what are your guiding principles? What are your concrete objectives? Who can you count on as part of your team? What do you need to focus on?

The answers to those questions will help you build healthier relationships in your personal and professional lives. Healthy teams, trusting community relationships, and networks of support create a virtuous cycle in your life. Instead of leading with concern and anxiety, spewing negativity over things you can't control, you can stand solidly in your Circle of Influence. You can cultivate balance and peace in your life, trust others, and lead with love.

CHAPTER 8

LEADING WITH LOVE

"If you want to change the world, go home and love your family."
—MOTHER TERESA

I went through a hard time my junior year of high school. My girlfriend and I were having trouble, and it was really getting to me mentally. Later on when we broke up, I wound up in a full-blown depressive episode, but at the time we were just struggling along. I remember sitting on my front porch with my head in my hands, lost in thought and feeling terrible.

I heard our front gate open, and looked up to see my baseball coach coming up the walk. His route home from the ball field took him down my street, and when he saw me he stopped the car. He sat down beside me and asked what was wrong.

He already knew that something was bothering me, because he could see it in my playing. Once you learn the mechanics of pitching and have built up muscle memory for the correct technique, it becomes a mental game. I was definitely off my form, and Coach Korn wanted to know if there was anything he could do to help. We had a long conversation and I told him all my troubles. I don't recall his advice, but it meant a lot that he took the time to sit and listen to me.

He was tuned in to me and what I needed. It mattered to him whether or not I was doing well, for my own sake. He was paying attention, not just to my performance on the field, but to how I was feeling inside.

That's the essence of leading from your heart, with love. A leader achieves results with and through other people, but they also achieve results *for* people and *in* people. Your team members aren't a means to an end. They are individuals who have unique perspectives, responses, and needs.

LEAD FROM THE HEART

A leader needs a big, bold vision to inspire people, but once you make your Leader's Algorithm public, it isn't just *your* vision anymore. You create a relationship of accountability with your team and your stakeholders. Your vision impacts them. It depends on them. It must include their needs and their best interests. That vision of their needs and concerns, what matters to them, gives them a place in your heart.

When I look back on why I became a teacher, and then why I became an administrator, the focus has always been to make a positive difference in students' lives. When I consider why I became a superintendent, the answer is the same: it was a way to make a bigger impact on the future of my students. In each domain where I was given influence—from a single social studies department, to overseeing curriculum and instruction, and all the way up—each step was an opportunity to influence and help more of my fellow educators, so we could pursue excellence together. It's all about the relationships: with my students, with other teachers and administrators, with the community, and their relationships with each other.

At the same time, if you asked me what I would do over, that answer is also all about relationships! Ironic, isn't it? I could have focused more on social and emotional learning for our students. I could have invested more in my relationships with key stakeholders who held sway over our bolder initiatives. When you start to see everything through a heart-first lens, you see boundless opportunities to pour your heart into other people.

Great leadership is an act of love.

LOVE YOUR KIDS

The most important opportunity for a school leader is to pour your heart into the students in your district. When you take responsibility for students, they become yours. Every decision you make as an educational leader should be driven by one question: is it great for my kids?

When we have to make decisions about whether to close school, we wrestle with what's best for our kids. On one side, you may have hazardous weather conditions (or lately, hazardous health conditions). On the other, there's a lot more than academic instruction happening at school. We feed the students. We counsel them. We give them a safe place to be, and hopefully thrive. Those decisions aren't easy, so you have to bring the same diligence and prudence to them that you would for your own children.

I'm the father of two daughters. I would go through fire to make sure my children are well cared for and have the best opportunities in life. I want every student in my districts to have—to the best of my ability—every opportunity that my own daughters do.

At work, I always felt a strong connection with the custodians, the security workers, and the food service staff because I saw my mom and dad in them. When it came to my students, I saw *myself* in them. I know what I went through as a child, two generations removed from my grandparents in Puerto Rico who couldn't read or write in their own language. I know the traumas and struggles I dealt with, and many of the students in my districts had similar stories.

I didn't have a rigorous foundational education. My teachers weren't focused on excellence; they were just teaching to their supervisors' mediocre expectations. I was a good kid who did my work and didn't cause problems, so they left me alone. I got good grades, but I wasn't challenged. When I made it to Yale, I struggled. There were really big, obvious gaps between the preparation I got in school and the preparation that my suburban and private school classmates had received.

That's not good enough for my students. One of my fundamental beliefs is that children should not be doomed to a life of poverty and struggle because they were born into a certain zip code. Their family's socioeconomic status is going to impact their life, but it should not limit their educational opportunities. It should not cut them off from being prepared for good jobs or higher education if they want it. School districts should not trap students in a cycle of ignorance and deprivation, but should uplift every single one of them by giving them the tools they need to be successful.

Public education is the strongest mechanism we have as a society to fundamentally transform the trajectory of a family, to fulfill the proverbial American dream. Life can make you cynical, and working in the public school system can make you even more cynical. But when I look at the kids in my district—my kids—I see all the possibilities of what their lives could become.

I hope you see it, too.

Love your students like you love your own children.

A *VERY* PERSONAL THEORY OF ACTION

In Chapter One, I referred to the TOA you'll create for your work as a "personal TOA." Now that we've talked about life balance and pouring your heart into people, let's make it really personal. I want to challenge you to think about the most important difficulties and conflicts in your own life with the same framework. Where do you struggle to lead with love in your personal relationships? What situations are hard to walk into heart-first?

Two of my biggest challenges happened in the same year. My twenty-five-year marriage was ending, and my mother-in-law was dying.

These two events were intertwined, because my mother-in-law had been in my life for over thirty-one years. She was always kind and generous toward me, and I loved her dearly. She was also my daughters' grandmother, so regardless of the legal status of my marriage, she was family. The tension of family grief and the tension of estrangement made it very difficult for everyone to navigate.

Earlier, we discussed how you need good models to learn leadership, and you need to model good leadership for others. Here, I needed mentoring on how to conduct myself. My daughters needed me to model showing love in difficult circumstances.

I needed a solid Theory of Action. I already knew some of my guiding principles, because I keep my personal mission statement in my journal:

- Care about others.
- Be honest.
- Love my family.
- Respect humanity.
- Be humble.

I turned to my mother. As usual, she gave me wonderful advice. She reminded me of something my grandmother Cecilia (her own mother) had said when she was terminally ill. She asked my mom to call her whole family—children, sisters, in-laws, nieces, nephews, grandchildren, everyone who was living. "Tell them to come see me now to say goodbye," she said, "and if they can't come now, don't bother to go cry at my grave."

My mom went on to say, "You're not divorcing your mother-in-law. She has always been very good to you, so you need to go pay your respects while she's still living."

She was right. So my daughters and I traveled to Connecticut to celebrate Chanukah at the family gathering at my mother-in-law's home, with all the aunts and cousins on that side of the family. It was just as awkward and emotional as you might expect, but when we were ready to leave, I pulled my daughters aside.

I told them, "Listen, it's almost time for us to go, and I'm going to ask for a private moment for the three of us with Bubbe. We are Muñozes. And what Muñozes do is pay our respects to people before they die. We go up to the person, we tell them we love them. We tell them all the wonderful things we appreciate about them. If there's anything you need to ask forgiveness for, you ask it. If there's anything you need to forgive, you forgive it, because you want the person who's passing to go with a happy heart and a clear conscience."

That's exactly what we all did. Then we kissed her and said goodbye.

It would have been so easy to skip the whole thing. I had every excuse in the world to drop my daughters off for the holiday meal and distance myself. Fortunately, I also had my mom, my grandmother, and all the caring leaders who had poured into my life, pushing me to lead with my heart.

I needed those great models to remind me who I am and what's most important to me. Then I could remind my daughters of who they are. Together, we were able to grow a little bit closer to the best version of ourselves.

PUTTING IT TOGETHER

Because of those experiences, I drafted a *very* personal Theory of Action to guide me forward in life's ongoing challenges. I theorize that:

If I focus on these actions:

1. Live with purpose and intentionality
2. Tell the truth and do not fear the results of that truth
3. Conduct myself with patience, kindness, generosity, loyalty, and self-discipline
4. Work hard to grow my knowledge and understanding
5. Use my talents for the greater good

If I move toward this objective:

To make those closest to me secure, happy, and proud in our loving relationships; and to teach, serve, give, and comfort others.

If I commit to these guiding principles:

1. Care about others
2. Be honest
3. Love my family
4. Respect humanity
5. Be humble

Then I will live a life of significance, success, love, and joy.

How about you? What are your guiding principles in life? What is your ultimate goal?

A VISION OF LOVE

When you put other people's needs in the center of your work, it remakes your whole vision of leadership. When you identify with the people you serve, it ignites a passion to serve them well that can carry you through all sorts of challenges. That passion to help others flourish will guide you to relationships and actions that bring your vision to life.

The eyes of love transform your view of work, teams, community, and your own life.

CONCLUSION

"Give the world the best you have, and it may never be enough; give the world the best you've got anyway."

—MOTHER TERESA

At the beginning of this book, I asked you to consider how you would define leadership for yourself, and to write a personal Theory of Action. Now, I want to share a secret with you: my own Leadership Algorithm for this book.

I offered you a guide to personal development that would transform your life, work, and relationships. My Theory of Action is that:

- *If* I focus on bridging the gap between formal training for educational leaders and the hands-on practice of leadership in the real world;
- *If* my book is read by educators, administrators, and superintendents who desire to grow their leadership skills;

- *If* we achieve a critical mass of educational leaders who share a philosophy of excellence and heart-first leadership; and
- *If* we all commit to certain guiding principles

Then as a team, we can transform not only our individual life, work, and relationships, but the lives, careers, and families of millions of students across this nation.

What are those guiding principles?

1. Excellent leadership requires intentionality, execution, and accountability.
2. Leading with vision requires bold action.
3. Leading with high expectations elevates everyone.
4. Leading through teamwork means relying on your whole team to reach your goals.
5. Leading with skills requires ongoing, rigorous development for everyone (especially the leader).
6. Leading in your community means cultivating trusting relationships with all your stakeholders.
7. Leading with resilience requires support, boundaries, and a balanced life.
8. Leading with love means reminding people of who they are, so they can become the best version of themselves.

So, team, how are we doing?

I'm serious. This Leadership Algorithm depends on you to be part of the feedback loop. Please feel free to contact me with questions or comments at: **pablo@themunozcompany.com**.

In order for us to achieve our ultimate objective of transformational leadership, there are a number of specific actions you'll need to take to execute this TOA.

First—because it's so urgent—if you are struggling with your mental health or physical effects from the stress of your job, please get help. Don't wait for a moment of crisis. You can't do it alone, and you don't have to. Reach out to the people around you who are ready, willing, and able to give you practical and emotional support. Make a plan to delegate. Learn to set boundaries. Order your own priorities for balancing your life.

Next, if you haven't yet done the exercises in Chapter One, Chapter Five, and Chapter Six to develop your leadership definition, your personal TOA, your leadership story, and your community political map, get started! These are projects that need time and consideration. The more you think deeply about these questions and return to them over time, the more they will benefit you. Most of all, I urge you to contemplate your vision for your own future, and the daily mission that will make it come true in your life.

We spoke in earlier chapters about the **3 Ls** of Love, Laser-like focus on teaching and learning, and Leadership. Now I'd like you to consider a **fourth L: Legacy**. As I reached the end of my tenures at Elizabeth and Passaic, and particularly now that I look forward to sharing these lessons with you, I want to emphasize that legacy is not about awards or recognition. At the end of the day, the most important question is, "What have you done to improve the lives of children?"

For me, knowing that the improvements my team and I made have deep roots that will persist is the heart of my professional legacy. In my personal life, the way I've led, taught, and influenced my daughters is the legacy I cherish most. My life will live on after I'm gone in the lives of all these children.

Finally, in order to achieve critical mass, we need to share these ideas and this book with others. Use it for your graduate school program. Discuss it with your colleagues and your team. Share it with your family and friends. As you put these ideas into practice, explain why you're making changes and why they matter.

If you'd like me to come into your district to consult on leading with excellence, please get in touch! We all need to work together to make our ultimate goal a reality. You can find out more about my services and access other resources at **www.themunozcompany.com**.

To be trusted with a leadership position is a tremendous honor and an opportunity to make a lasting positive impact on the world. My vision is to elevate every student's opportunity—every student, in every district—for a healthy, happy, successful, and meaningful life. My mission every day is to develop leaders who can bring that vision to pass.

Let's do it together. Will you join me?

ACKNOWLEDGMENTS

Thank you to my team at Lioncrest who took a chance on me and made this book possible: my publishing manager Esty Pittman, my executive editor Brannan Sirratt, as well as Emily Anderson, Rachel Brandenburg, Jennifer Burnside, Ian Claudius, Harlan Clifford, Ellie Cole, Eden Crawford, Matthew DePonceau, Emily Ellis, Rose Friel, Jennifer Glover, Skyler Gray, Caroline Hough, Dan Johnson, Rikki Jump, Vi La Bianca, Greg Likins, Frances Jane O'Steen, Bianca Pahl, Mariano Paniello, Soups Pryce, Maggie Rains, Robert Roth, Benito Salazar, Emily Sisto, Natalie Sowa, Lex Statzer, Tara Taylor, Lindy Taylor, Neddie Ann Underwood, Jericho Westendorf, and Carmela Wright. A special thank-you to Kristen Holsman-Francoeur for spending many, many hours with me to collect my thoughts and experiences for this book. I thank you for your compassion during my crying episodes. My sincere gratitude goes to Ellen Seltz, my incredible writing partner, for your ability to see and capture my vision for the book.

I thank the Elizabeth and Passaic boards of education and staff for their support and for allowing me to lead. Thank you to Rafael Fajardo and Raúl Burgos for helping me become a superintendent of schools. Special thanks to Craig Miller, who encouraged me to document our work. I hope you enjoy the book.

Thank you to my mentors. Herb Hennessy, rest in peace. Thank you for noticing me at Yale and encouraging me to become a teacher. Ray Korn, thank you for being an outstanding coach who taught me how to excel at baseball, leadership, and life. Tim Quinn, thank you for the foreword and for your mentorship and guidance. Gary Schaer, thank you for clearing the way so I could lead. You are a kind, compassionate, and professional gentleman. Gordon MacInnes, thank you for recommending me to The Broad Academy. It's incredible how your short email changed the course of my career and life. And thank you to The Broad Academy for teaching me how to be a superintendent of schools.

Thanks to the many colleagues who read drafts of my manuscript and gave me good advice: Raúl Burgos, Michelle Calas, Donna Coen O'Gorman, James Coyle, Michael Cummings, Keith Furlong, Elise Genao, Rachel Goldberg, Donald Goncalves, Thomas Hatch, Michelle Keith, Gordon MacInnes, George E. Mikros, Brian G. Osborne, Carlos Rodriguez, Joel Rose, Charles B. Sampson, David Sciarra, Gary S. Stein, Jeffrey Truppo, Dilcia White, and Brian Zychowski.

A leader needs a strong, talented team to have success. Thank you to my teams in Elizabeth and Passaic: Erlinda Arellano, Jennifer Barrett, Michelle Calas, Eveny de Mendez, Aida Garcia,

Rachel Goldberg, Donald Goncalves, William Greene, Olga Hugelmeyer, Maria Infante, Harold Kennedy, James Shoop, Mabel Torres, Jeffrey Truppo, and Dilcia White, as well as Jerome Dunn, Stephen Liddawi, and Annie Rooney, may they rest in peace. Special thanks to Donald, Jeffrey, and Rachel for helping me create this book.

Now I turn to my family. *For me, family is the most important relationship in life.* Some will argue this point, saying that "family *and* friends, not family *or* friends. That family *or* friends is a false dichotomy. You can have strong relationships with both family *and* friends." And I would not argue with that. But life experiences have taught me that family is more important than friends. Friends come and go, but throughout my life, during happy and dark times, wins and losses, achievements and failures, during the birth of my children and the death of loved ones, my family was always there. I can't say the same for friends.

So let me pay tribute to my family who have supported me every day. Some are still with me and some are not.

Mamá, Cecilia Nieves, rest in peace. My grandmother who raised me was the strongest and smartest woman I have ever met. I miss you.

Lidia Bonet, Carlos Morales, Johnny and Ivonne Nieves—my aunt and cousins who lived for many years in the same house as me, and always loved and supported me. Tía Lidia, thank you for being my second mother. Carlos, Johnny, and Ivonne, thank you for being my brothers and sister. A special shout-out to Ivonne who was with me during dark times as my life was turned upside down.

Doris, Alyssa, and Taylor, my sister and nieces: thank you for your love and support. Doris, I love you and I don't tell you that enough.

Mami and Papi, Mom and Dad. You love me unconditionally. I hope I made you proud of me. I'm certainly proud of you. I love you.

Cecilia and Sadie, my daughters who are twenty-one and eighteen as I write this. I love you unconditionally. I'm so proud of you both and the fantastic women you have become. Your life will be a roller-coaster ride, but in the end I'm sure you will be happy and filled with joy.

Thank you, Alanna, for inspiring, encouraging, and believing in me. For thirty-one years, the influence of your thinking and your presence in my life made me a better man.

APPENDIX A

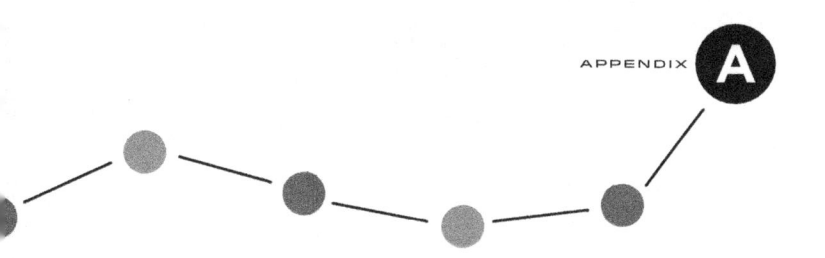

PERSONAL THEORIES OF ACTION

ELIZABETH PUBLIC SCHOOLS

Pablo Muñoz
Superintendent of Schools

MY THEORY OF ACTION

March 12, 2012

If I lead with a focus on three actions:

1. Keeping the school system focused on its vision and mission in an effort to produce excellent results
2. Selecting effective leaders to carry out the mission
3. Getting the resources into the classroom

If I select leaders that focus on six items:

1. Vision
2. Mission
3. Increasing student learning and achievement by improving the instructional core
4. Teamwork
5. Trust
6. Loyalty

If I get the school system to commit to Managed Instruction by:

1. Creating and implementing an aligned, coherent, and detailed curriculum
2. Providing a world-class workforce of effective teachers and leaders

3. Providing a comprehensive professional development system
4. Providing frequent formative and summative assessments
5. Providing a comprehensive student information system
6. Providing interventions for students, teachers, and schools
7. Measuring performance and applying predetermined consequences

If I get the school system to commit to the 3 Ls guiding principles:

1. Love
2. Laser-like focus on teaching and learning
3. Leadership

Then our students will graduate prepared to pursue a college education; will think, learn, achieve, and care; and will receive high pay in the 21st century marketplace.

PASSAIC PUBLIC SCHOOLS

Pablo Muñoz
Superintendent of Schools

MY THEORY OF ACTION

July 31, 2018

If I lead with a focus on three items:

1. Keep the school system focused on its vision and mission in an effort to produce excellent results
2. Select effective leaders to carry out the mission
3. Get the resources into the classroom

If I select leaders that focus on six items:

1. Vision
2. Mission
3. The Instructional Core
4. Teamwork
5. Trust
6. High Expectations

If I move the district toward an *Aligned Instructional System*:

1. Create and implement aligned, coherent, and detailed curricula
2. Develop effective teachers and leaders driven by a culture of high performance
3. Provide a comprehensive professional development system

4. Set clear standards and measure progress through formative and summative assessments
5. Build a comprehensive student information system
6. Establish interventions for students, teachers, administrators, and schools
7. Measure performance, progress, and growth

If I develop the school system through the **2 Qs** guiding principles:

1. **Quantity:** We must provide more opportunities for significant student learning, including: after-school, Saturdays, and summers; productive use of classroom time; community partnerships; and digital learning platforms
2. **Quality:** Define what is effective teaching and leading, so that we provide frequent and meaningful feedback, evaluation, and professional development

Then we will create a top-tier school system that prepares our students to attend college and to earn high pay in the 21st Century marketplace.

APPENDIX B

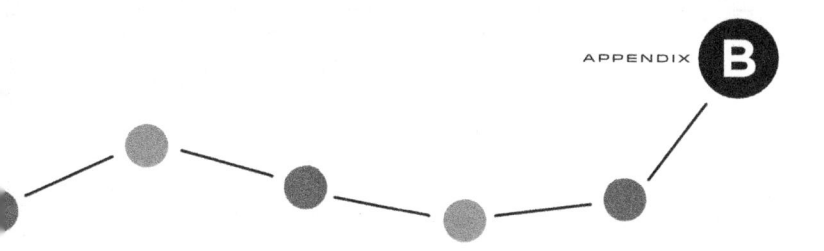

EXAMPLES OF CORPORATE VISION AND MISSION STATEMENTS[14]

---

14   Sources: Company websites and annual reports.

COMPANY	VISION	MISSION
AT&T	To be the best broadband provider in the United States.	To create connection—a connection to friends, family, work, commerce, education, health, entertainment, and more.
CVS	We are working to deliver a superior health care experience for consumers to improve health outcomes and lower costs, supporting individuals for every meaningful moment of health throughout their lives.	We help people with their health wherever and whenever they need us.
EXXONMOBIL	We are committed to being the world's premier petroleum and chemical manufacturing company.	We develop and apply next-generation technologies to help safely and responsibly meet the world's growing needs for energy and high-quality chemical products.
GENERAL ELECTRIC	To adapt and innovate solutions to three of the world's most pressing challenges: the future of smarter and more efficient flight, precision healthcare that personalizes diagnoses and treatments, and the energy transition to drive decarbonization.	We rise to the challenge of building a world that works.

COMPANY	VISION	MISSION
GENERAL MOTORS	Our vision for the future is a world with zero crashes, zero emissions, and zero congestion.	To invest in electric vehicles (EVs) and autonomous vehicles (AVs), software-enabled services and subscriptions and new business opportunities, while strengthening our market position in profitable internal combustion engine (ICE) vehicles.
GOOGLE	We aspire to give everyone the tools they need to increase their knowledge, health, happiness, and success.	To organize the world's information and make it universally accessible and useful.
MICROSOFT	To enable digital transformation for the era of an intelligent cloud and an intelligent edge.	To empower every person and every organization on the planet to achieve more.
PEPSICO	To be the global leader in beverages and convenient foods by winning with PepsiCo Positive (pep+).	Create more smiles with every sip and every bite.
PROCTER & GAMBLE	We're committed to making peoples' lives better in small but meaningful ways, every day.	We will provide branded products and services of superior quality and value that improve the lives of the world's consumers, now and for generations to come.
UPS	To be the world's premier package delivery company and a leading provider of global supply chain management solutions.	Customer First, People Led, Innovation Driven

APPENDIX C

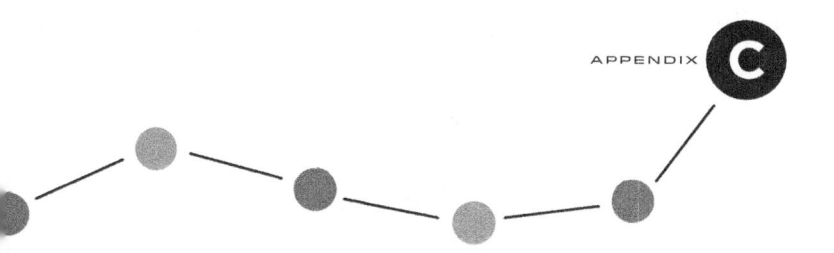

EXCERPT FROM CAFR FOR ELIZABETH PUBLIC SCHOOLS, 2012

MAJOR INITIATIVES

During the 2011–2012 school year, the Elizabeth Public Schools continued to act upon its mission of providing excellent educational experiences and services to inspire every student to think, to learn, to achieve, and to care. The district implemented the grants and initiatives funded to the Board of Education in the most effective manner to improve student achievement and to prepare all students for postsecondary education as is stated in our district's core beliefs and commitments.

Many educational experiences and services were provided during the past twelve months to support our students' efforts to meet the Common Core Curriculum Content Standards, and to successfully handle both the state and the school system's standardized assessments thereby impacting the types of programs that we implemented and the manner in which each was put into practice.

THE 3 Ls

The implementation of grants and initiatives during the 2011–2012 school year, based heavily upon achieving our district's vision and mission to improve student achievement, was driven by high expectations and our **3 Ls: Love, Laser-like Focus on Teaching and Learning,** and **Leadership**.

LOVE

Along with setting high expectations, our **3 Ls** serve as the foundation upon which we build our core business of teaching and learning. The first L, **Love,** is vital to the Elizabeth Public Schools. For our professional community to truly achieve excellence, our schools, offices, and community must treat each other well and embrace the vision of becoming one of the best school systems in America. Love is about creating a caring environment that is most conducive of our core business.

The Elizabeth Public Schools' commitment to creating a loving and caring environment is best summed up by the district's Pledge of Ethics. The Pledge, as introduced to the district in 2005–2006, continued to be a hallmark of proper conduct within the district's school buildings and central offices during 2011–2012. The Pledge asks members of the Elizabeth Public Schools Professional Community to treat people as they wish to be treated, understand that the school community is a "special place," listen to others respectfully, speak in a calm voice, dress appropriately, inspire the best in oneself and others, care about others, and be a lifelong learner. The Pledge has helped to change our district's culture and increase staff morale by treating people well.

The district's efforts to increase safety and discipline also fall in line with the first L, Love. The successful implementation of the school uniform policy continued in 2011–2012. Between the 2006–2007 and 2011–2012 school years, we have added nearly every school to the uniform program, including over 23,000 students. It is anticipated that within the next year, all district schools will be implementing the use of school uniforms. Research has indicated that the use of school uniforms has a positive impact on student achievement and student discipline.

With the threat of security challenges unfortunately a part of present-day America, the district worked hard during the 2011–2012 school year to keep its Crisis Response Plan as realistic, all-encompassing, up-to-date, and usable as possible. Updated crisis information was provided to all schools and offices. District Crisis Team meetings were held regularly and district crisis training was ongoing.

The Elizabeth Board of Education implemented the AlertNow automated messaging service, which allows Elizabeth Public Schools to alert large numbers of people (parents/guardians or staff) instantly in the case of an emergency or a special event. The system was a valuable tool during 2011–2012 as it allowed the district to successfully notify parents about events such as school closings, fitting sessions for school uniforms, and Early Childhood registration.

In harmony with new antibullying legislation that was passed by the State of New Jersey, the Elizabeth Public Schools created the "No Bully Zone" in 2011. The "No Bully Zone" was created to help eliminate bullying in the district's schools. A web page was created on the district website for the "No Bully Zone" that offers resources to parents and students about preventing bullying and respecting others.

Another aspect of creating a safe, warm learning environment is ensuring our students are well nourished to prepare them for learning. Students throughout the district are provided breakfast each morning, which studies have shown increases attentiveness and energy throughout the school day. Additionally, the Elizabeth Public Schools has collaborated with the Alliance for a Healthier Generation to help promote better food choices for its students. The Alliance for a Healthier Generation is a partnership with the William J. Clinton Foundation and the American Heart Association, which works with public school districts around the country to promote healthy schools programs. As a result of this effort, Elizabeth Public Schools has adopted strict nutritional guidelines in which the sugar, calorie, and fat content of all foods served are thoroughly analyzed. In fact, twenty schools in the district have already been designated as *National Healthier Schools*.

The Elizabeth Public Schools, in collaboration with the Gateway Regional Chamber of Commerce and Trinitas Regional Medical Center, also hosted a "Healthy Leap into Summer" health expo for high school students. This annual health expo is the largest teen obesity awareness program in the nation, according to the United States Department of Health and Human Services. The one-day program promoted healthy lifestyles to high school students while addressing the epidemic of teen obesity. At the event, more than one thousand high school students participated in workshops, health screenings, and interactive health exhibits, and received samples of healthy foods and snacks.

LASER-LIKE FOCUS ON TEACHING AND LEARNING

The second L, **Laser-like focus on teaching and learning**, underscores the importance of keeping our attention on our core business while preparing all students for postsecondary education. Having a laser-like focus on teaching and learning is most significant in the classroom where our students are being inspired to think, to learn, to achieve, and to care.

Success in this endeavor has provided excellent results for the Elizabeth Public Schools. The highlight of this success in 2011–2012 is two of our high schools, Elizabeth High School and Alexander Hamilton Preparatory Academy, being ranked among the best high schools both in the state and nationally by several media outlets. Elizabeth High School received ranks of Number 2 in New Jersey and Number 77 in America from the *Washington Post*; Number 6 in New Jersey and Number 139 in America from *US News & World Report*; and Number 217 in America from *Newsweek*. The 2012 rankings marked the second year in a row Elizabeth High School was ranked Number 2 in New Jersey by the *Washington Post*. Alexander Hamilton Preparatory Academy made their debut in the high school rankings in 2012, receiving ranks of Number 46 in New Jersey and 1,421 in America from *US News & World Report* and Number 65 in New Jersey and 1,444 in America from the *Washington Post*.

Laser-like Focus on Teaching and Learning in the Elizabeth Public Schools begins with a rigorous and comprehensive curriculum. One of the critical elements of the curriculum is Language Arts Literacy. The district's Early Literacy Program continued to flourish this past year as individual students were provided targeted help in the primary grades by specially trained staff. During the 2011–2012 school year, prekindergarten classes for three- and four-year-olds were available both in district and in partnership with local childcare providers. All classes were taught by certified staff and class sizes were kept small with no more than fifteen students to each teacher. Training in the High/Scope Approach to Early Childhood Education was provided to all new Early Childhood staff, along with refresher courses for more experienced professionals. The High/Scope approach to preschool education enables young children to take initiative and develop their social, intellectual, and physical capacities.

Elizabeth Public Schools continued to implement the language arts literacy program in kindergarten through fifth grade with an emphasis on phonemic awareness, phonics, fluency, vocabulary, and text comprehension. This program is designed to support students' efforts to become competent readers as early as possible in their school careers, with the goal of having students reading at grade level by the third grade. We believe that literacy skills are vital to student success in school and in their lives and every student must read at or above grade level.

Children in grades K–3 who scored in the lowest 25 percent on formative and summative assessments were provided various interventions including tutoring. Students identified as in need of this intensive and specifically focused assistance received small group instruction. Teachers were trained to diagnose the areas of difficulty of the student and to assist them with overcoming these roadblocks in order to foster their learning and to help them stay on level with the rest of the class in the area of reading development.

The language arts literacy program in grades four to nine, Literacy is Essential to Adolescent Development and Success, or LEADS, is thematic based and consists of multiple writing tasks and project-based learning. The LEADS program continues to provide intensive training in basic reading skills and emphasizes the art of writing, introducing our young readers to high-quality classic and contemporary children's literature. Our literature series features the literary works of a diverse field of authors that teaches the valuable concepts of reading, writing, and grammar while also introducing life and culture lessons. In addition, at the high school level, creative writing and technical writing courses were created to help students enhance their writing and usage of language.

In addition to providing our students with the best possible opportunity to learn to read early and well, it is our hope that our literacy programs will develop a passion for the written and spoken word in all of our students. We also aim to promote social awareness through literary instruction and to develop the idea of reading as a lifelong pursuit.

Another critical element of the curriculum is mathematics. Students are now being offered a more advanced and rigorous mathematics program to prepare them for competition in the global marketplace once they leave our school system. In 2011–2012, algebra continued to be a required course for all eighth-grade students. This step will provide freshmen at our six high schools with the tools to take geometry during their first year.

Many excellent educational experiences took place in the area of science in 2011–2012.

Dr. Albert Einstein Academy School No. 29, a NASA Explorer School (NES), continued its partnership with the National Aeronautics and Space Administration in a program that features science, technology, engineering, and mathematics.

The work begun in 2008 through our partnership with the Merck Institute for Science Education (MISE) Academy for Leadership in Science Instruction, continued to help achieve the nation's STEM (science, technology, engineering, mathematics) educational goals. The goals of the Academy are to build a vision of effective science instruction; to deepen teachers' knowledge and develop effective leadership skills to improve science instructional practice, curriculum, and assessment in their schools; and to share these practices with colleagues via targeted outreach.

The NJIT Pre-Engineering program at Dwyer Technology Academy offers students a rigorous program of mathematics, science, and technology courses that provide hands-on experiences to enable students to connect what they learn in school to different branches of engineering.

One of the commitments of the Elizabeth Public Schools is to prepare every student for postsecondary education. The district is meeting that commitment by offering excellent educational experiences through unique educational programs.

Dr. Orlando Edreira Academy School No. 26 applied and was accepted to become an International Baccalaureate (IB) school beginning in the 2011–2012 school year. IB schools offer continuous international educational experience from early childhood to preuniversity age. A sequence of two programs—the Primary Years Programme and the Middle Years Programme—provide a consistent structure of aims and values and an overarching concept of how to develop international-mindedness.

The Advancement Via Individual Determination (AVID) program continued at Hamilton Preparatory Academy and expanded in 2011–2012 to PK–8 schools. In 2011–2012 the AVID program was introduced at Schools 2, 6, 13, and 28. AVID is a research-based instructional model that encourages students to prepare for and participate in a challenging college preparatory curriculum. In addition to enrolling in Honors and Advanced Placement level courses, students will receive academic support through a specially designed AVID elective, taught by AVID-trained instructors.

Three of our high schools have partnered with the National Academy Foundation (NAF), a proven educational model that includes industry-focused curricula, work-based learning experiences, and business partner expertise. John E. Dwyer Technology Academy offers the Academy of Information Technology and the Academy of Engineering; Thomas A. Edison Career and Technical Academy offers the Academy of Hospitality & Tourism; and Admiral William F. Halsey Jr. Leadership Academy offers the Academy of Finance.

The RUBY (Rutgers University Business for Youth) program gives promising sophomore students the opportunity to experience a career in the financial world. RUBY consists of ten two-hour sessions held weekly that introduce students to careers in finance. Under the tutelage of instructors, students listen to a brief lecture and are separated into teams. Beginning with conducting market research, they develop, step by step, business plans for companies that they create. Activities lead to a competition at the conclusion of RUBY where students present their business plan to judges through the use of PowerPoint and websites that they build to determine the winner of the best business plan. Juniors who were in the program as sophomores serve as surrogate mentors for the incoming group of twenty-five sophomores participating in RUBY the following year while their own new curriculum addresses topics such as preparing for and financing college.

The excellence in preparing students for postsecondary education was reflected on the report cards of many high school students. Select high-performing high school students received a voucher for two tickets to a New Jersey Devils hockey game as part of the New Jersey Devils Honor Roll Program. High school students who made the honor roll during the first marking period of the 2011–2012 school year were rewarded with the voucher for their commitment to educational excellence. There were 356 high school students among the six high schools in the district to receive the voucher award.

An important part of teaching and learning is creating a well-rounded student. Elizabeth Public Schools also helped to create excellence in athletics and the arts. Sports clinics were provided in the fall and spring to children in grades K–8 to help develop and enhance athletic abilities. Students were offered clinics in golf, gymnastics, swimming, tennis, and volleyball to learn more about the fundamentals and to promote interest in participating in those sports. Throughout the district, students performed in the New Jersey State Troopers Top Physical Challenge and in Trooper Youth Week to develop higher physical fitness levels. Elizabeth Public Schools achieved excellence in athletics as several athletes earned All-Union County honors from the *Star-Ledger*, including boys tennis player Jorge Rodriguez Del Ray who became the first Elizabeth tennis player to win a Union County Tournament in nineteen years and was named the *Star-Ledger* Union County Player of the Year. Additionally, Elizabeth High School's football, boys soccer, and boys basketball teams all competed in the North Jersey, Group 4, Section 2 championship game with the boys basketball team winning the sectional crown.

To help create excellence in the arts, the Elizabeth Public Schools continued to implement the Arts Institute as an after-school program during 2011–2012. Children who participate in the Arts Institute are instructed in areas such as visual and performing arts, public speaking, and forensics to develop and enhance their artistic abilities. The Elizabeth High School Instrumental Band once again enjoyed the excellent educational experience of playing side-by-side with the New Jersey Symphony Orchestra to an audience of elementary Elizabeth Public Schools students. Students from throughout the district had their artwork selected for exhibition at the All-State Touring Show of the Union County Teen Arts Festival. The Elizabeth Public Schools, through its partnership with the Summit Visual Arts Center of New Jersey, provides high-quality arts education and exhibition programs. The Arts Center is devoted exclusively to contemporary art through studio classes, workshops, special programs, and exhibitions. For the second time in 2011, the Elizabeth Public Schools produced a Holiday Celebration Show, highlighting student performances from schools throughout the district, which was aired during the holiday season on Cablevision.

Another important part of teaching and learning is the need to boost student performance on state tests. The Elizabeth Public Schools conducts quarterly benchmarking and benchmark assessments in all content areas. A diagnostic approach is taken and interventions are put in place to ensure that all students are performing proficiently and at grade level. Test preparation was also streamlined into language arts and mathematics through the development of a benchmark system, which allowed classroom instruction to be continuous. The 2011–2012 assessment results proved positive as student proficiency increased in almost every grade level.

In keeping with the Keys to Excellence Strategic Plan guidelines, the district continued to host an after-school program from October through May at various school locations. Participants received assistance from teachers in the areas of reading, language arts, and mathematics. Teachers also helped students master all-important test-taking strategies in preparation for both state (NJ ASK and HSPA) and district (Terra Nova and NJ PASS) assessment programs.

Teaching and learning in the Elizabeth Public Schools is enhanced significantly through the use of technology. Elizabeth Public Schools' technology initiative continued with impressive results. We have implemented over four thousand iPads throughout the district, in addition to expanding the number of laptops that have been placed in all of our K–12 schools to equip students with computers to learn how to use different software programs while learning and completing assignments. SMART and STAR boards, a whiteboard that connects and interacts with computer technology, can be found in over 80 percent of our schools, including our early childhood centers, to provide students with innovative lessons in all subject areas.

Record-keeping responsibilities of both teachers and administrative staff have increasingly been integrated with technology, resulting in improved data collection. The Elizabeth Public Schools continued to use a robust, district-wide Student Information System (SIS) known as Pearson's PowerSchool® Premier in 2011–2012. The technology is essentially an avenue for administrators, team members, parents, and students to access important information regarding day-to-day activities. The secure system allows users to access information such as absences, tardiness, grades, test scores, assignments, medical and guardian alerts, birthday reminders, transportation information, school activities, and student schedules. The system went live for administrators during the 2007–2008 school year and was made accessible to students and parents beginning in 2008–2009. Pearson's Inform program was also integrated in 2009–2010, which is used more specifically for student assessment data collection and analysis.

The district's Help Desk again handled staff questions and problems concerning computers and network issues. For questions and concerns from members of the greater community, Elizabeth Public Schools implemented its customer service website EPS Direct that is dedicated to meeting the needs of our parents, guardians, and residents.

A redesign of our district website has made following the news and events of the Elizabeth Public Schools easier than ever. The new system empowered each school building to continually update and provide the latest information about their school. In addition, the district maintains an Elizabeth Public Schools Facebook page; YouTube channel; and EPS TV, an Internet site that streams live Elizabeth Public Schools events, leveraging the strength of social media to broadcast information to a larger audience.

LEADERSHIP

Finally, our district will achieve excellence with effective **Leadership**, the third L. The 2011–2012 school year began with the Welcome Back Administrators event that offered two full days of professional development. Great attention was paid to providing the district's administrative staff with the skills and knowledge necessary to effectively serve as educational leaders. The Keys to Excellence Council continued its work in implementing and communicating the vision, mission, and core beliefs of the Elizabeth Public Schools throughout the district. Keys to Excellence

Leadership Cohorts, led by members of the Council, functioned as professional learning communities and peer networks to develop instructional leaders across the district.

The work performed through our partnership with the Panasonic Foundation has yielded three major support systems to achieving excellence in our schools:

- Instructional rounds have been instituted as a way for us to evaluate and prescribe instructional practices that will bring student success. The process has included central administrative staff observing educational practices in several district schools and providing analysis essential to the continued improvement of student performance.
- Teaching and Learning Team visits allowed administrators to support schools in strengthening the instructional core, identify staff needs, and provide professional development to school staff.
- Finally, Assistant Superintendent Walk-Throughs were conducted as another layer of support and observation to support teaching and learning through guidance, direction, and evaluation, while holding schools and principals accountable for their contributions to academic success.

These three major support systems are built on the foundation of school-level ninety-day plans and a shared definition of rigorous instruction. The school-level ninety-day plans provide a framework for monitoring progress, refining and revising strategies, and informing next steps while a shared definition of rigorous instruction provides a concrete, observable description of rigorous instruction that can be used as the basis for fine-tuning and improvement of instruction that spans all grades and subjects.

The district continued its in-district professional development program, the Institute of Teaching and Learning, in 2011–2012. The Institute for Teaching and Learning provided over 300 hours of professional development opportunities during the summer, after school, and weekends. Teachers continued to receive professional development training focusing on instructional strategies and how to implement them in the classroom curriculum. These workshops were provided by Elizabeth Public Schools staff development employees who themselves have had extensive training and experience.

The Elizabeth Public Schools also participated in the New Jersey Network of Superintendents, a diverse group of New Jersey superintendents in a community of practice to develop their understanding of instruction and their work as system leaders. By supporting the development of the superintendents' understanding of the instructional core, the network sought to foster system-wide changes in the superintendents' districts, and, ultimately, contributed to improvements in student achievement for all students, particularly students of color and students living in disadvantaged communities.

The Elizabeth Board of Education continued to effectuate change in educational policy. The Board is provided a quarterly report that identifies performance measures and accountability. Through a partnership with the Center for Reform of School Systems (CRSS), the Board uses the quarterly data and works with a CRSS facilitator to develop strategies of reform aligned with the latest successful educational models. The Board, as dictated in district policy, conducts quarterly management oversight workshops with Elizabeth Public Schools' instructional and operation departments who provide the Board with a deeper understanding of the operations of their respective departments on a daily basis.

OUR LEARNING CENTERS

Modernizing and constructing school buildings and providing our students with warm learning environments require strong leadership that will fight for the rights of our students. The Elizabeth Public Schools and the Elizabeth Board of Education continued to implement its landmark decision to restructure and realign the school district in 2009–2010. John E. Dwyer Technology Academy, Thomas A. Edison Career and Technical Academy, Elizabeth High School, Admiral William F. Halsey Jr. Leadership Academy, Alexander Hamilton Preparatory Academy, and Thomas Jefferson Arts Academy all officially opened their doors as independent high schools for the first time in September 2009.

In 2010-2011, the Elizabeth Public Schools and Elizabeth Board of Education commenced its newest district restructuring, "Blueprint 2: Expanding Excellence for Everyone." This initiative included creating an extended day environment for Schools 1, 2, 5, 6, 13, and 28, expanding the Gifted and Talented program by adding 400 students in grades 2–8 to the program at Terence C. Reilly School No. 7, closing School No. 17, and adding preschool classrooms for 465 more students by using Blessed Sacrament Church, St. Hedwig Church, and St. Adalbert Church as annexes for Schools 1, 5, and 16.

In 2011–2012, the "Accelerating Excellence" initiative was adopted, resulting in extending the instructional day at twelve neighborhood schools. The extended day schedule starts at 7:30

a.m. and concludes at 3:45 p.m. As a result of this initiative, all PK–8 schools in the district operated on an extended day schedule. Additionally, the Board of Education entered a long-term agreement for the use of St. Catherine's School. The facility was used to expand Alexander Hamilton Preparatory Academy, which provided new classrooms for 260 freshmen.

During the 2011–2012 school year, the Board of Education also continued its fast pace of providing new schools for our children. A groundbreaking for the new Elizabeth High School—Frank J. Cicarell Academy, which will be located next to Jefferson Arts Academy, was held in May 2012. The new high school was one of ten school construction projects approved by the New Jersey Schools Development Authority (NJSDA) among dozens submitted throughout the state in 2011. Construction was also continued on the new Victor Mravlag School No. 21 during 2011–2012. Throughout the year, district staff continued to work with the NJSDA to design future schools and to secure the necessary land on which to build the new facilities the district so desperately needs.

The 2011–2012 school year was rewarding for students and staff alike. Many steps were taken and initiatives launched that we feel will have a significant impact on student achievement in the years ahead.

APPENDIX D

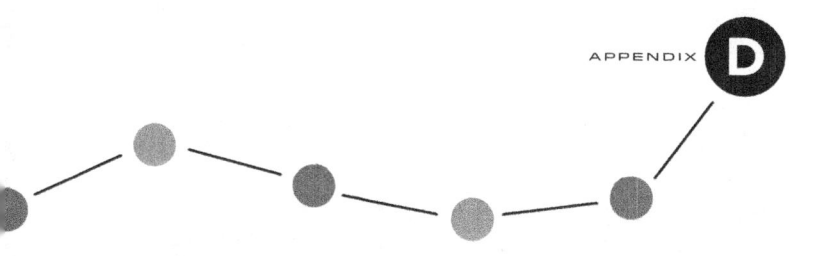

DATA DASHBOARDS

ELIZABETH PUBLIC SCHOOLS

Elizabeth Student Achievement Data Dashboard

	Students % Proficient						
	2005–2006	2006–2007	2007–2008	2008–2009	2009–2010	2010–2011	2011–2012
Kindergarten							
Reading	71	78	84	82	82	79	77
Language Arts	74	80	85	84	88		
Math	76	87	90	90	90	89	87
Grade 1							
Reading	75	76	81	81	83	75	78
Language Arts	78	77	84	83	84		
Math	73	74	81	86	87	84	83
Grade 2							
Reading	58	61	66	71	75	74	78
Language Arts	78	78	83	82	88		
Math	73	76	78	81	84	82	86

Elizabeth Public Schools changed for grades K–2 the TerraNova test edition in 2011. TerraNova 2nd Edition was used 2004–2010; TerraNova 3rd Edition was used 2011–2012.

Grade 3							
Language Arts	69	75	80	51	49	53	56
Math	78	80	82	69	72	71	67
Grade 4							
Language Arts	66	69	74	44	41	47	47
Math	71	76	80	62	65	73	71

NJ DOE changed the proficiency standards in Language Arts Literacy and Mathematics for grades 3 and 4 in 2009.

Elizabeth Student Achievement Data Dashboard

	Students % Proficient						
	2005–2006	2006–2007	2007–2008	2008–2009	2009–2010	2010–2011	2011–2012
Grade 5							
Language Arts	73	73	42	46	49	39	44
Math	70	73	68	71	70	68	74
Grade 6							
Language Arts	49	54	33	52	48	52	49
Math	48	66	55	60	62	68	71
Grade 7							
Language Arts	57	56	43	50	54	44	42
Math	38	39	47	51	55	56	52
Grade 8							
Language Arts	42	45	57	63	66	71	72
Math	30	34	37	48	50	55	62

NJ DOE changed the proficiency standards in Language Arts Literacy and Mathematics for grades 5, 6, 7, and 8 in 2008.

Elizabeth Student Achievement Data Dashboard

	Students % Proficient					
	2005–2006	2006–2007	2007–2008	2008–2009	2009–2010	2010–2011	2011–2012
Grade 9							
Language Arts	▓	▓	62	65	71	67	72
Math	▓	▓	39	44	50	55	62
Grade 10							
Language Arts	▓	▓	63	63	67	66	71
Math	▓	▓	49	49	53	64	66

Elizabeth Public Schools began administering the NJ PASS in grades 9 and 10 in 2008.

Grade 11							
Language Arts	58	61	56	63	68	74	80
Math	45	37	44	43	49	50	63
Grade 11 (Banked)							
Language Arts	66	73	68	76	78	81	NA
Math	52	52	52	55	61	62	NA

At the high school level, students were administered the HSPA multiple times until they passed both sections for graduation. As a result, the NJ Department of Education began using up to three test administrations per student to calculate AYP. These results are the "Banked" results from the spring of the year indicated. When this data dashboard was created, we did not have three test administrations for the cohort of students tested in the spring of 2012.

Elizabeth Student Achievement Data Dashboard

	Students % Proficient						
	2005–2006	2006–2007	2007–2008	2008–2009	2009–2010	2010–2011	2011–2012
Science							
Grade 4	57	60	66	75	83	77	85
Grade 8	47	46	58	64	64	69	71
Early Childhood							
Average ECERS-R	4.96	5.3	5.6	5.46	5.67	6.14	6.34
High School							
% Completing in 4 years	74	70	79	74	75		
Accountable School						67	61
Attending School						60	67

The New Jersey Department of Education changed the Graduation Rate calculation formula in the 2010–2011 school year. The new Graduation Rate was reported by attending school and by accountable school. Attending school is inclusive of only students who are attending one of our in-district schools. Accountable school includes the out-of-district-placed students' data at the school of record for each student.

Average SAT Score	1201	1190	1201	1229	1171	1205	1246

The 2005–2006 school year marked a change in the SAT test. During this year, a third component (Writing) was added, thus increasing the total possible points to 2400.

# of SAT Exams Scored	464	502	480	465	316	720	623

Average AP Score	2.2	2.1	2.1	1.8	2.1	2.0	2.0

Advanced Placement (AP) tests are scored on a 5-point scale (from 1–5). College credits may be awarded for scores of 3, 4, and 5.

# of AP Exams Administered	194	469	465	752	726	963	1355

PASSAIC PUBLIC SCHOOLS

Passaic Student Achievement Data Dashboard

NJ DOE changed the state exam to PARCC in 2015 and to NJSLA in 2019. No testing in 2019–2020 due to COVID-19.

	Students % Proficient					
	2013–2014	2014–2015	2015–2016	2016–2017	2017–2018	2018–2019
Grade 3						
English Language Arts		14	21	23	30	29
Math		22	26	25	31	32
Grade 4						
English Language Arts		21	25	30	32	35
Math		24	25	26	24	27
Grade 5						
English Language Arts		22	23	29	31	30
Math		24	23	24	21	24
Grade 6						
English Language Arts		23	25	29	33	33
Math		23	25	25	20	16
Grade 7						
English Language Arts		20	32	33	36	42
Math		18	21	13	13	19
Grade 8						
English Language Arts		19	33	40	37	37
Math						

Grade 8 math exam not administered. Grade 8 students take Algebra I or Geometry exam.

Passaic Student Achievement Data Dashboard

NJ DOE changed the state exam to PARCC in 2015 and to NJSLA in 2019. No testing in 2019–2020 due to COVID-19.

	Students % Proficient					
	2013–2014	2014–2015	2015–2016	2016–2017	2017–2018	2018–2019
Grade 9						
English Language Arts		14	23	19	13	25
Algebra I		18	18	24	12	11
Grade 10						
English Language Arts		11	20	18	23	25
Geometry		4	10	3	15	7
Grade 11						
English Language Arts		17	23	24	16	21
Algebra II		5	8	11	6	13

Algebra I, Geometry, and Algebra II exams are taken by students in grade 7 through high school.

Passaic Student Achievement Data Dashboard

	2013–2014	2014–2015	2015–2016	2016–2017	2017–2018	2018–2019
Early Childhood						
Average ECERS-3			4.33	4.79	4.82	4.91

2015–2016 provided new baseline for future comparison; this includes mathematics and science in instrument.

	2013–2014	2014–2015	2015–2016	2016–2017	2017–2018	2018–2019
High School						
% completing HS in 4 years	77	79	77	81	81	71

The minimum credits requirement for high school graduation beginning with the class of 2019 increased from 120 to 150 credits.

	2013–2014	2014–2015	2015–2016	2016–2017	2017–2018	2018–2019
SAT Participation	295	263	384	524	669	1256
Advanced Placement (AP)						
Enrollment	151	461	616	1175	1298	2158
Individual Students Tested	94	238	321	625	705	837
Total Exams Administered	145	370	511	987	1165	1507
Total AP Scholars	12	12	12	17	22	19
Exams Scoring 3, 4, or 5	35	110	115	140	220	254

Advanced Placement (AP) tests are scored on a 5-point scale (from 1–5). College credits may be awarded for scores of 3, 4, and 5. AP Scholars are students who have achieved the distinction of receiving a 3, 4, or 5 on three or more exams.

	2013–2014	2014–2015	2015–2016	2016–2017	2017–2018	2018–2019
Dual-Enrollment Courses						
Enrollment	263	219	412	559	908	1510

Dual-Enrollment courses provide students the opportunity to earn high school and college credits.

APPENDIX E

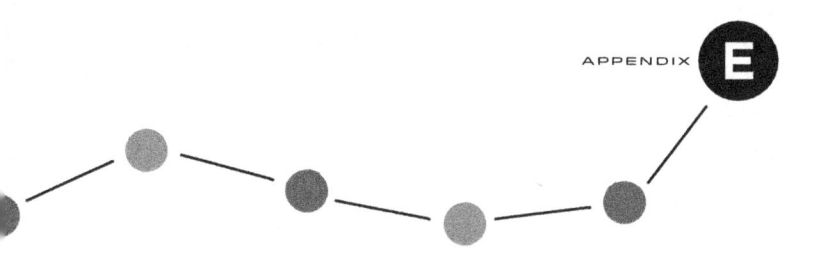

SUPERINTENDENT'S PLAN OF ENTRY—PASSAIC PUBLIC SCHOOLS, 2013

INTRODUCTION

I believe the Passaic Public Schools will be one of the best urban school districts in the State of New Jersey. We will work with incredible energy to accomplish this greatness by providing excellent educational experiences and services to prepare our students for college and careers. The Passaic Public Schools will create a path to greatness. We have an incredible and diverse staff and student body. Our focus is on improving student learning and achievement results, while pursuing excellence in athletics and the arts. I am excited about the possibilities that lie ahead.

I have spent my entire career in urban education as a teacher and administrator, including over eight years as a Superintendent of Schools. I plan to take a fresh look at everything that touches our district. The Plan of Entry period allows me time to listen and learn from all stakeholders in order to create a great school system.

The activities outlined in this Plan of Entry will take place during a three-month period of my leadership transition. The plan set forth below is designed to approach a myriad of complex issues facing the current Board, staff, stakeholders of the district, and me, the newly appointed Superintendent of Schools. As the three-month period progresses, I reserve the right to make modifications to the plan as conversations with stakeholders progress. This protocol allows flexibility in planning while offering a systematic plan of addressing the district's current challenges.

I strongly suggested that any stakeholder who might have ideas about how to improve upon the components of this plan write to me directly at pmunoz@passaic-city.k12.nj.us.

It should be noted that the Plan of Entry work occurs simultaneously with the responsibility of operation of the school district. The obvious duties of day-to-day operations and problem solving are in full course while entry takes place.

CULMINATION OF THE PLAN

Upon successful completion of the intended actions in this plan, I will report to the members of the Board my proposed agenda.

GOVERNANCE TEAM

Objectives:

1. Establish the Board and Superintendent as a cohesive governance team with a student-centered teaching and learning agenda.
2. Build a positive, productive, and trusting working relationship with individual Board members and the Board as a whole.

Activities:

1. Schedule an individual meeting with each Board Member for one-on-one perspective.
2. Establish a clear understanding of roles, responsibilities, expectations, and systems for mutual accountability.
3. Establish a regular communication system with the Board.
4. Review the Board of Education meeting agenda and reports.
5. Discuss current and determine future use of Board committee structure and roles and responsibilities.
6. Review the Board of Education election calendar.

ORGANIZATIONAL CAPACITY AND ALIGNMENT

Objective:

1. Establish a strong teaching- and learning-focused district executive team.

Activities:

1. Schedule one-on-one meetings with key central office staff to determine how each person will be supportive of dramatic improvement to student achievement. Also, ask them, "How effectively do we/you deliver on preparing our students for college and careers?"
2. Develop an action plan for the development of the district's Strategic Plan.
3. Review current or anticipated vacancies in central office staffing and develop a plan for filling these positions.
   A. Two Assistant Superintendents
   B. High School Principal
   C. Middle School Principal (evaluate and determine renewal or nonrenewal)
4. Establish a cabinet and schedule meetings.
5. Study policies, regulations, job descriptions, and table of organization.
6. Request a briefing paper from all direct reports providing an overview of their current area of responsibility; a list of major initiatives underway with timelines; a list of major accomplishments and awards; a list of significant or potential problems in each area of responsibility and how they are resolving them; and a list of major decisions that need to be made in one month, three months, and six months.

7. Review résumés of staff in top district positions and request a list of their top ten responsibilities.

STUDENT ACHIEVEMENT

Objectives:

1. Analyze patterns in student achievement data and the gap in advancement between various student populations in order to determine an appropriate course of action for teaching and learning.
2. Raise expectations for all students.

Activities:

1. Review student assessments for all student populations.
2. Review current or anticipated vacancies in school staffing and develop a plan for filling these positions.
3. Review district curriculum and programs of study.
4. Review after-school and Saturday programs.
5. Review student attendance, promotion/retention, grading, and high school graduation policies.
6. Assess current professional development program, paying particular attention to current capacity and the training needs of principals, teachers, and cabinet. Develop a plan for the development of aspiring leaders and new administrators.
7. Meet with each principal to discuss the performance of students and staff; to review School Improvement Plans and School Performance Reports; to determine how each principal will be supportive of dramatic improvement to student achievement; and to ask them, "How effectively do we/you

deliver on preparing our students for college and careers? How do you improve teaching and learning?"
8. Review implementation status of teacher, principal, and vice principal evaluation systems.
9. Review status of Student Growth Objectives (SGOs) and administrators' goals.
10. Schedule classroom visits and instructional walk-throughs for the school year; and observe instruction with principals.
11. Listen to teachers in grade level and department meetings.
12. Meet with school leadership teams.

COMMUNITY AND PUBLIC RELATIONS

Objectives:

1. Establish positive working relationships with civic leadership, community leadership, and other community agencies.
2. Establish the role of each employee union/association as advisor and partner to the Superintendent.
3. Increase opportunities to promote the District programs with the community and enhance advocacy for the District's needs and mission.
4. Ensure ongoing, clear, and consistent communication with all stakeholders.
5. Establish a positive working relationship with representatives of the media.

Activities:

1. Ask each Board Member to suggest three to five names of community organization leaders, and subsequently, to arrange meetings between the Superintendent and these leaders.

2. Meet with local and state elected officials.
   A. Mayor
   B. Assemblyman
   C. City Council members
3. Meet with the Passaic Executive County Superintendent.
4. Meet with the Regional Achievement Center (RAC) director.
5. Plan for roundtable meetings with key constituency groups.
6. Meet with union leaders.
7. Meet with PTA/PTO presidents, and discuss parent meetings.
8. Plan for meetings with foundation, nonprofit, and philanthropic organizations.
9. Establish roundtable meetings with staff and high school students.
10. Review the public information plan.
11. Attend meetings of key organizations, such as chambers of commerce, Rotary, and other suggested organizations throughout the year.
12. Meet with the community of faith leaders.

OPERATIONS AND FINANCE

Objective:

1. Understand the current strategies, strengths, and opportunities for improvement in the District's operations and finance.

Activities:

1. Review the district's Quality Single Accountability Continuum (QSAC) self-assessment and supporting documentation.

2. Review Harassment, Intimidation, and Bullying (HIB) reports and procedures.
3. Review district's information technology system and plan.
4. Meet with the Schools Development Authority (SDA) leaders regarding new construction and grant projects.
5. Review status of construction projects, Long-Range Facilities Plan, maintenance plan, and school facilities checklists.
6. Review district's financial projections, resource allocation, budget, audits (e.g., CAFR), and management letters.
   A. School
   B. Central office
   C. Federal—No Child Left Behind (NCLB) and Individuals with Disabilities Education (IDEA)
   D. Early Childhood Program Aid (ECPA)
   E. Special Education Medicaid Initiative (SEMI)
7. Review all district pending legal proceedings.
8. Review the district's safety, security, and emergency plans.
9. Review process and timeline for budget development.
10. Review Curriculum Audit and create a plan to address the findings and recommendations.
11. Review the school year calendar.
12. Create a phone chain list for emergencies and school closings.
13. Review the current procedure for inclement weather school closings.

Made in United States
North Haven, CT
31 May 2024